PATRICK MOORE'S
STORY OF THE
EARTH
FOR THE UNDER TENS

PATRICK MOORE'S
STORY OF THE
EARTH
FOR THE UNDER TENS

PHILIP'S

Acknowledgments

My thanks are due to Dr Peter
Cattermole, for some very helpful
comments, and to Paul Doherty, for
his excellent illustrations. I am most
grateful to them.

PATRICK MOORE
Selsey

Illustration acknowledgements

Peter Cattermole p. 12; NASA p. 37;
The Natural History Museum, London
pp. 14–15 bottom, pp. 18–19 top, p. 19,
pp. 22–23, p. 25.

© Patrick Moore 1991

British Library Cataloguing in
Publication Data
Moore, Patrick *1923–*
    Earth for the under tens
    1.   Earth (Planet)
    I.   Title
    525

ISBN 0–540–01210–6

CONTENTS

CHAPTER 1
THE EARTH – OUR HOME

The Earth is our home in space. Men have lived here for tens of thousands of years, and should be able to do so for many millions of years to come. We have the right sort of air, the right sort of temperature, and enough water. There is nowhere else in our part of the universe where we could live under natural conditions.

What I hope to do, in this book, is to give you an outline of what we know about our world – its nature, its history and its future. Much of the time we will be dealing with geology, which is the science of the Earth itself, but we will also have to touch upon astronomy, the science of the sky; meteorology, the science of the air; and of course chemistry and biology. All these studies are linked together.

We must turn first to astronomy, and see just where we belong in the universe. Early men believed the world to

Our Galaxy is a typical spiral galaxy, with a bulge in the centre and 'arms'.

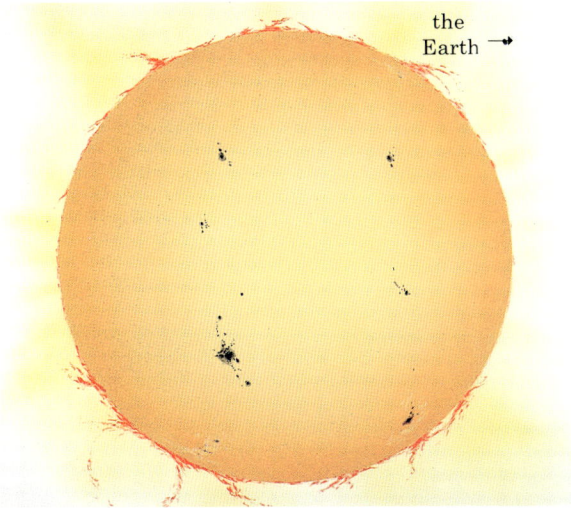

The Sun and the Earth. The arrow at the top of the picture points to our planet which is tiny compared to the star.

be flat, which was natural enough; after all, it really does look flat, apart from the usual hills and valleys. But long before the time of Christ it had become known that the Earth is a globe, spinning round on its axis once in 24 hours. Next it was found that the Earth is an ordinary *planet*, moving round the Sun; it is a member of the Sun's family or Solar System. It takes 365 days to complete one full journey round the Sun.

The Earth's distance from the Sun is 93,000,000 miles (150,000,000 kilometres). This may sound a long way, and of course this is true, but it does not seem much to an astronomer, who has to deal with distances so great that nobody can hope to understand them. If you could get into a car and drive straight from the Earth to the Sun, moving at a steady 55 miles per hour (88 kilometres per hour), which is the speed limit for cars in the United States of America, the journey would take you 193 years.

The Sun is a *star*. It is no larger or hotter than many of the stars you can see on any clear night, and it appears so brilliant only because it is so much closer to us. The nearest star beyond the Sun lies in the southern part of the sky, and is known as Proxima Centauri (unfortunately it can never be seen from Britain, because it does not rise above our horizon). Drive straight from the Earth to Proxima, at our speed of 55 m.p.h., and you will find that you will have to be ready for a journey lasting for 52,000,000 years. All the other stars are even further away.

Our star-system, or *Galaxy*, is made up of about 100,000 million stars, every one of which is a sun. As well as the stars, we can see huge clouds of dust and gas which we call *nebulæ*. These are of great importance when we come to look at the way in which the Earth was born. Beyond our Galaxy we can see others, so that our system is by no means the only one.

Now let us come back to the Sun itself. It is so large that its globe could hold more than a million Earths; its diameter is 865,000 miles (1,390,000 kilometres). Unlike the Earth, it is not solid. It is made up of gas, and it is very hot indeed. Even its surface has a temperature of almost 6000 degrees Centigrade, which is why it is dangerous to look straight at the Sun through any telescope or even a pair of binoculars.*

The Sun is not 'burning' in the usual meaning of the word, but as I will explain in Chapter 3 it is sending out energy all the time, and we depend upon it for all our light and heat. Even the Moon, which looks so brilliant at night-time, shines only by reflecting the rays of the Sun.

* I have given a warning about this in *Astronomy for the Under Tens*, the first book in this series.

7

CHAPTER 2
HOW THE EARTH MOVES

The Earth is not a perfect globe, but is slightly flattened at the poles, as shown in the diagram. The diameter as measured through the equator is 7926 miles (12,753 kilometres), but the polar diameter is only 7899 miles (12,709 kilometres), so that the Earth is shaped like a slightly squashed orange. The reason for this is that the Earth is spinning round once in 24 hours, making the equator bulge out.

It is this spin which gives us our day and night. In the next diagram the Earth's axis is marked by the line NS, N marking the north pole and S the south pole. Because the Earth spins from west to east, the Sun seems to rise in an easterly direction and set toward the west.

The Earth's rotation makes it bulge out slightly at the equator, so that its equatorial diameter is 27 miles (44 kilometres) more than its polar diameter.

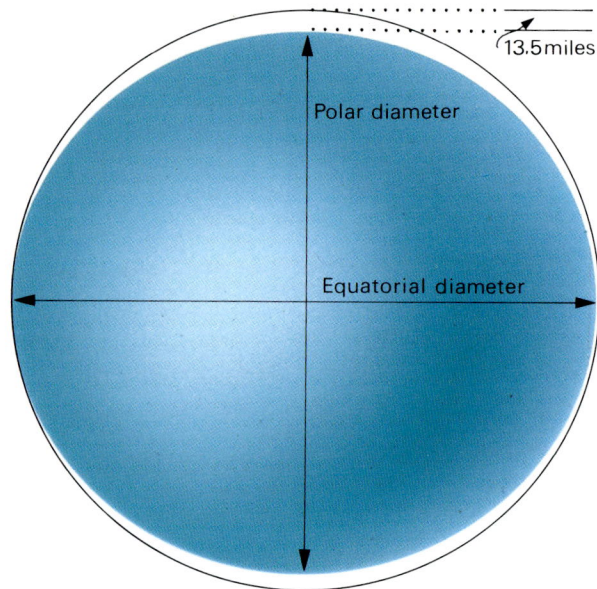

13.5 miles

Polar diameter

Equatorial diameter

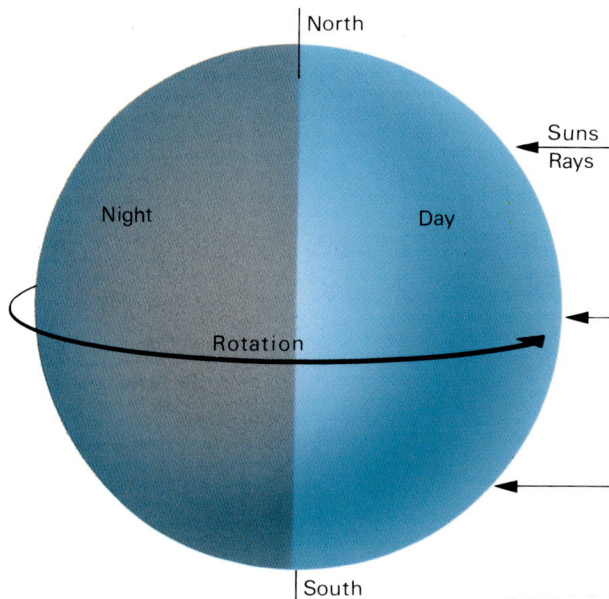

North

Suns Rays

Night

Day

Rotation

South

The Earth's rotation gives us day and night. Because the Sun's rays fall on the Earth from one direction only, one half of the planet is in daylight and the other half in darkness at any one time.

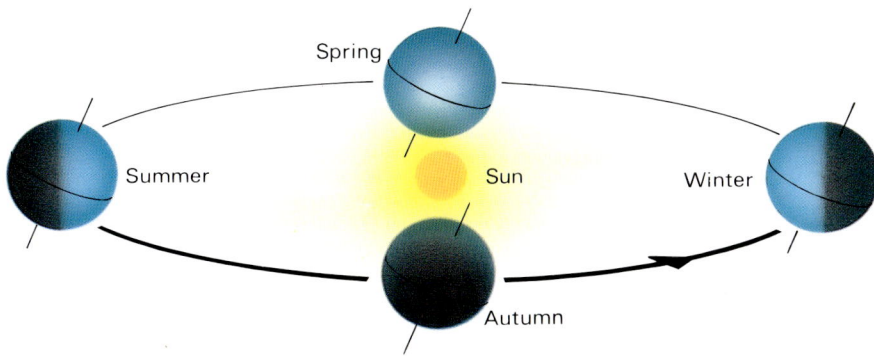

The tilt of the Earth's axis combined with its orbit around the Sun causes our seasons.

The days and nights are not equal in length all through the year, because of the effect of the seasons. The Earth does not stand 'straight up' in its path or orbit round the Sun; the axis is tilted at an angle of $23\frac{1}{2}$ degrees.

Look first at the position during northern summer (around June). The Sun's rays are coming down directly on to the northern part of the Earth, and the north pole N is in sunlight all the time. London lies well north of the Earth's equator, and is marked in the diagram by L. As the Earth spins, it is easy to see that L will be on the daylight side of the world longer than the time it will spend on the dark or night side. In the southern part of the Earth, the positions are reversed; the south pole (S) has no daylight at all.

In northern winter (around December) the Earth is tilted in the other direction. Now it is the south pole which is in daylight, while the north pole is in darkness; in London, the 'nights' are longer than the 'days'. During late March and late September, at the time of the *equinoxes*, the London days and nights are equal in length at 12 hours each.

It is this tilt of the axis which causes the seasons. It is rather surprising to find that we are actually at our closest to the Sun in December, when the distance is $91\frac{1}{2}$ million miles (147 million kilometres) as against $94\frac{1}{2}$ million miles (152 million kilometres) in June; the Earth's orbit is not quite circular. However, this changing distance does not have much effect upon the seasons.

The Earth takes one year to complete a full journey round the Sun. In fact the true 'year' is $365\frac{1}{4}$ days, and this makes our calendar less straightforward than it would otherwise be. Our familiar 365-day year is a quarter of a day too short. In four years, therefore, the error has added up to a complete day, and unless we did something about it we would soon find that the calendar had become 'out of step', with Christmas falling in the middle of the northern summer. The way to avoid this is to add an extra day to the calendar every four years. In 'leap years' the shortest month, February, has an extra day added, giving it 29 days instead of the usual 28.

The Moon, our companion in space, moves round the Earth (it is the only natural body to do so), taking just over 27 days to make a full journey. Because it depends upon reflecting the light of the Sun, it shows apparent changes of shape from new to full. Generally, there is one new moon and one full moon every month.

CHAPTER 3
THE EARTH'S BEGINNING

It used to be thought that the Earth could be no more than a few thousands of years old. This is quite wrong. We can find fossils – the remains of dead animals and plants – which are much older than that. By now we are fairly sure that the age of the Earth is about 4600 million years.

To find out just how it was born, we must look back still further. I have already mentioned nebulæ, which are large clouds of dust and gas in space. Stars are formed inside these nebulæ, and our Sun certainly began as a spinning cloud of material. This material collected together, because of the action of the force of gravity, and slowly the Sun was built up.

All matter is made up of atoms, which are amazingly small. There are 92 different kinds of atoms known in the universe, and these are known as elements. Iron, gold, silver and copper; for example, are elements; water is not, because one atom-group or molecule of water is made up of a mixture of two elements, hydrogen and oxygen. Each molecule contains two hydrogen atoms together with one atom of oxygen, which explains the famous chemical formula H_2O.

Hydrogen is the lightest and commonest of all the elements, so that the original nebula contained a great deal of it. As the cloud shrank, it became hotter near its centre. At last the temperature reached about ten million degrees Centigrade, and this had a very important effect. The great heat, together with the pressure, made the

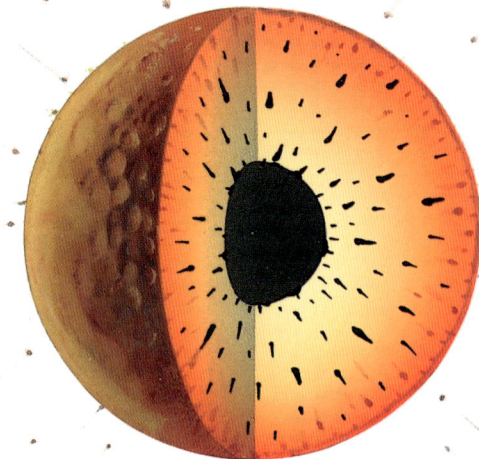

The Earth formed from a condensation in the cloud around the Sun and grew bigger by attracting other material towards it. The heavier elements sank and formed the magnetic core

hydrogen atoms run together to make up atoms of a slightly heavier element, helium. (To be correct, it was the centres or 'nuclei' of the atoms which ran together, but this need not bother us for the moment.) It takes four 'bits' of hydrogen to make up one 'bit' of helium. Every time this happens, a little energy is given off and a little mass (or 'weight', if you like) is lost. The Sun began to shine, losing mass at the rate of four million tons every second. This is still happening today, but I can promise you that there is no need for alarm; the Sun has so much hydrogen that it will not change much for many hundreds of millions of years yet.

In its early stage, the shrinking, spinning Sun was surrounded by a large cloud of material, much of which was hydrogen but which also contained heavier elements, including iron. Here and there the material in this cloud was denser than average, and so the material started to collect into separate lumps, each of which turned into a planet. As soon as a newly formed planet had become massive enough, it was able to pull in material from outside, so that it grew quite quickly.

A look at a plan of the Solar System shows that it is divided into two parts. The inner part contains four small planets: Mercury, Venus, the Earth and Mars. Then comes a wide gap in which move thousands of very small worlds known as minor planets or asteroids. Next we have four very large planets: Jupiter, Saturn, Uranus and Neptune, together with a small body, Pluto, which does not seem to fit into the general plan, and may not be a proper planet at all.

The four giants are not solid, but have surfaces made up of gas. They contain a great deal of hydrogen, and their solid centres are fairly small. The reason for this is that in the early story of the Solar System, the Sun 'blew away' most of the very light element hydrogen from the inner regions, so that the close-in planets lost most of their hydrogen and were left with only the heavier elements. Further away, where the temperatures were lower, the hydrogen was not blown away, so that the giant planets were able to hold on to it.

Slowly the Solar System turned into the sort of place it is today. The Earth was not yet solid and rocky, but was changing all the time.

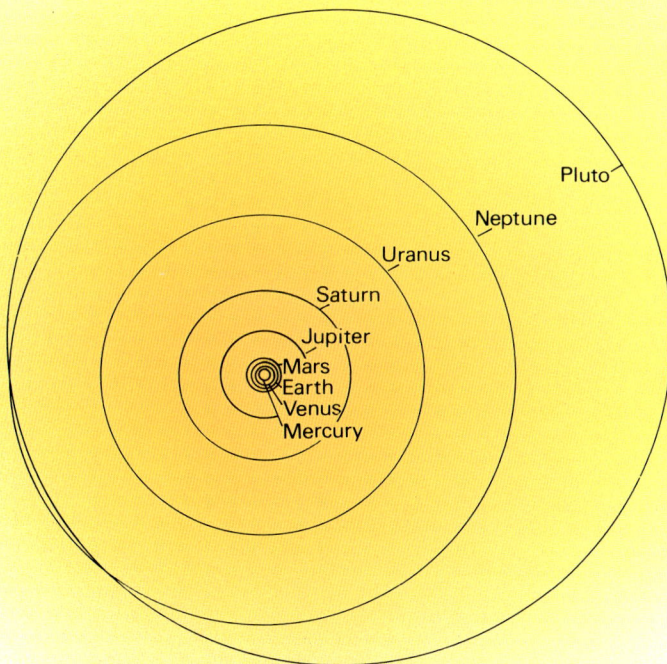

A plan of our Solar System showing the relative distances of the planets from our Sun.

CHAPTER 4
THE CHANGING WORLD

After several tens of millions of years, the Earth became cool enough for a crust to form. It was still shrinking, because of the effect of gravity, and it was also being bombarded by pieces of material which had been 'left over' when the large planets were growing. Each time a large rock hit the Earth some heat was added to it, and gradually this made the planet hotter inside once more. At last the heat was so great that iron, which is a heavy metal, began to melt and form droplets. These drops sank downward, so that slowly the Earth's core became very rich in iron together with another metal, the silvery-white nickel. Above the core there was rock which was less dense,

but was too hot to be solid, so that it could flow rather in the same way that treacle will do. This layer is known as the mantle. It contains a great deal of the lighter element silicon. The sand you see on the sea-shore is also made up largely of silicon.

Iron is magnetic, and the iron-rich core turned the Earth into a giant magnet. This was lucky, because the magnetic field protects us from dangerous radiations coming from space, and without it we could not live here.

When the Earth was first born, it had an atmosphere, but this atmosphere was not the same as that of today; most of it was made up of hydrogen. As we have seen, the Sun blew away much of the hydrogen, so that the Earth was stripped of its atmosphere, and for many

Ol Doinyo Lengai is an active volcano on the plains of Tanzania.

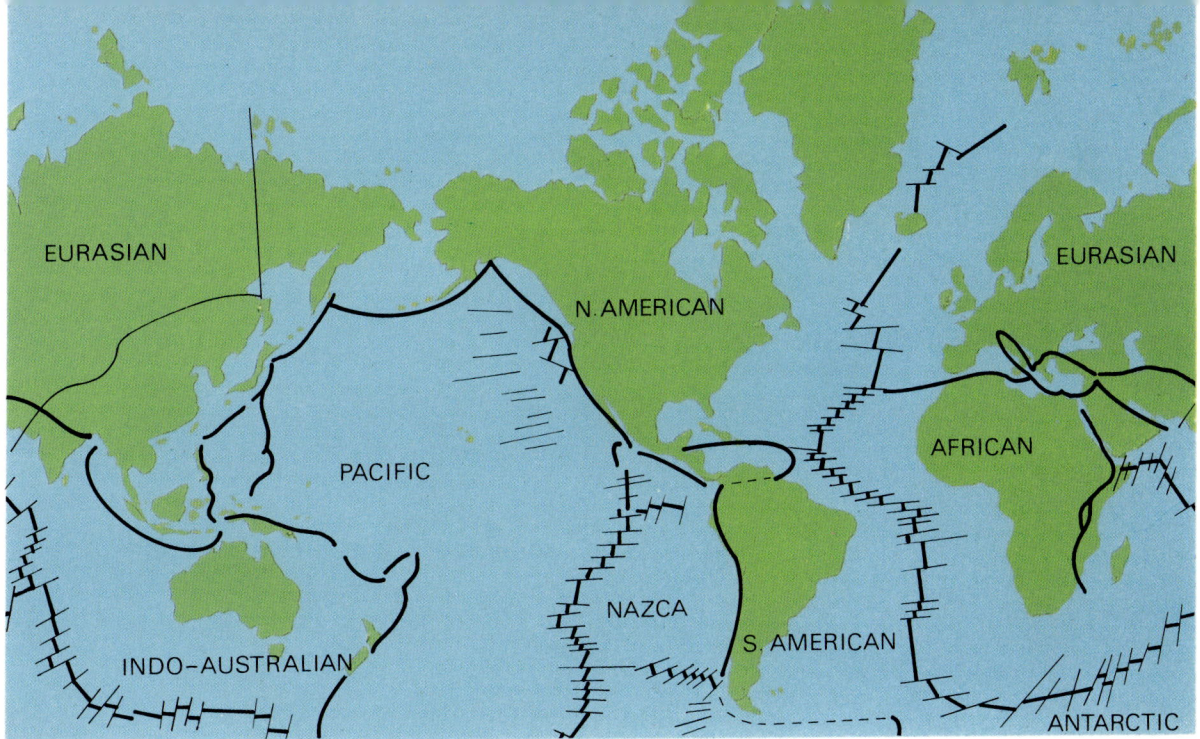

EURASIAN

N. AMERICAN

EURASIAN

PACIFIC

AFRICAN

NAZCA

S. AMERICAN

INDO-AUSTRALIAN

ANTARCTIC

The main fault lines between the Earth's plates.

millions of years it was airless. Then a new atmosphere was formed from gases sent out from inside the globe.

One reason for this was what is called 'radioactivity'. There are some heavy elements which change naturally into other elements, taking a long time to do so; while this is happening, heat is given off. One such element is uranium, the heaviest of the whole 92. Given enough time, it changes into a special kind of lead. This lead (not the same as the graphite in your lead pencil!) is slightly different from ordinary lead, and chemists can tell which is which. If, then, we find uranium together with special lead, the amount of the lead tells us how long the uranium has been there. It is this which makes us sure that the age of the Earth's oldest rocks is about 4600 million years. (There are other ways of studying this, too, but all give much the same answer.)

As the Earth's interior heated up,

there was tremendous activity. Volcanoes burst out; there were eruptions which sent out huge quantities of steam and other vapours, until a new atmosphere had been built up instead of the early hydrogen. It was still not 'air' which you or I could breathe, because it contained too much of the gas we call carbon dioxide and too little free oxygen, but there was enough water vapour to make clouds. Rain fell, and went on falling for long enough to form our oceans. Today more than half the Earth's surface is water-covered.

As the crust cooled and became thicker, it broke up into huge slabs or plates, which were pushed and pulled around on top of the moving, 'sticky' mantle. Parts of some of these plates became our continents, though at first they were arranged very differently from those of today.

The Earth was becoming ready for life. The lands were still unfriendly, but the oceans were different, and it was in the warm seas of the young Earth that life began.

CHAPTER 5
LIFE ON EARTH

In studying Earth history we depend mainly upon fossils, which as we have seen, are the remains of dead plants or animals. Soft parts will dissolve away, but bones and shells will not. There are also the footprints of long-dead creatures which have been left in rocks, just as you will leave foot-prints if you walk across wet sand; these are called 'trace fossils'.

We cannot be sure just when life began. The very earliest traces of it may date back for as much as 3500 million years, and we are fairly sure that there was simple life by 2000 million years ago, but it is not until about 590 million years ago that we come to the first proper fossils.

Neither are we sure just how life first appeared. All we can really say is that in some manner or other, non-living or 'inorganic' material was changed into true life. There have been suggestions that life on Earth was brought here from outer space, but most geologists prefer to think that it began in our own seas.

The first creatures were 'single-celled', and were very small. Then, about 590 million years ago, we come quite suddenly to sea life advanced enough to leave fossils.

Geologists divide the story of the Earth into different 'Eras', which are again divided up into different 'Periods'. The names are tongue-twisting, but it is best to get used to them at once, and there is nothing difficult about them once you have learned how to pronounce them. Here, then, is the geological time-scale:

Period	Millions of years ago Began	Ended	
PRE-CAMBRIAN ERA			
Archæan	3800	2500	Start of life.
Proterozoic	2500	590	Life in the seas.
PALÆOZOIC ERA			
Cambrian	590	505	Sea life.
Ordovician	505	438	First fishes.
Silurian	438	408	First land plants.
Devonian	408	360	Amphibians.
Carboniferous	360	286	First reptiles.
Permian	286	248	Spread of reptiles.
MESOZOIC ERA			
Triassic	248	213	Reptiles. Early mammals.
Jurassic	213	144	Age of dinosaurs.
Cretaceous	144	65	Dinosaurs, dying out at end.
TERTIARY ERA			
Eocene	65	38	Primates.
Oligocene	38	25	Development of primates.
Miocene	25	5	Modern-type animals.
Pliocene	5	2	Ape-men.
QUATERNARY ERA			
Pleistocene	2	0.01	Ice Ages. True men.
Holocene	0.01	Now	Modern men.

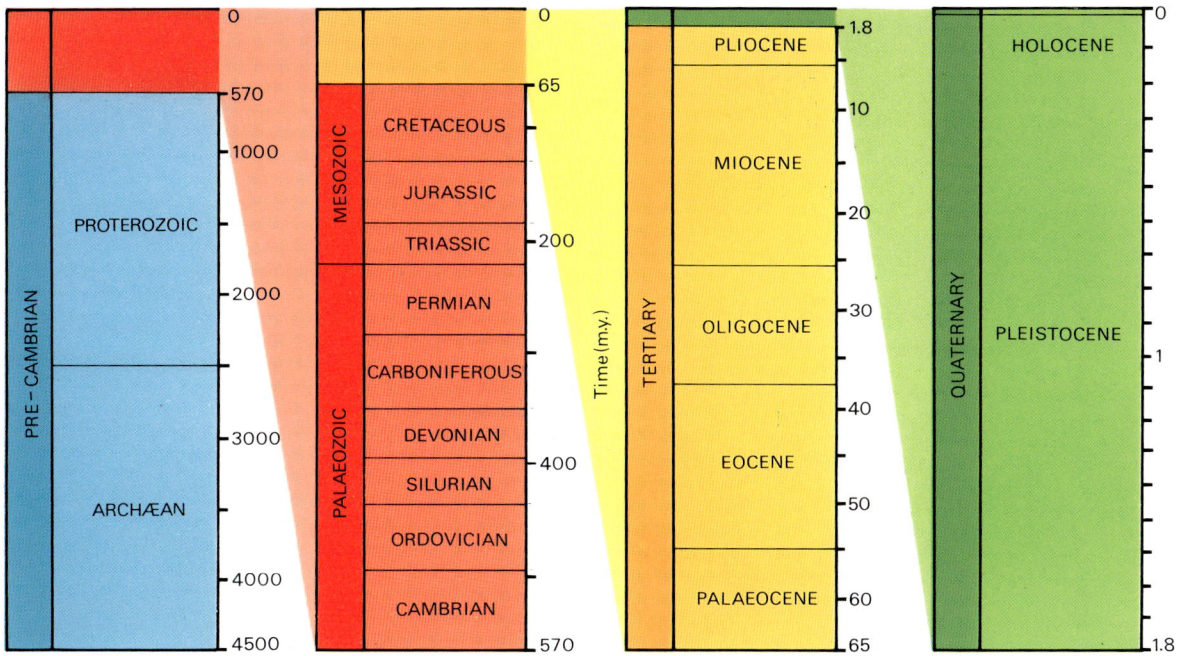

Geological time-scale. Starting at the bottom left it shows the relative lengths of the geological eras and periods. The different coloured section at the top of each column is shown in greater detail to the right.

The Holcene period, which is still going on, began only 10,000 years ago. This is not long when we remember how old the Earth is. To make this clear, let me give a time-scale in which the Earth's age is represented by one year, so that on this scale it was born on January 1. We can then fill in other parts of the story:

May 1:	First simple life in the seas.
October 20:	Spread of sea life.
November 20:	First fishes.
November 30:	First life on land.
December 7:	First reptiles.
December 12:	Dinosaurs.
December 15:	First mammals.
December 31:	5 p.m. First ape-men.
	11 p.m. First true men.

On this scale, the Romans left Britain less than one second ago. We are indeed newcomers to the Earth!

A patch-reef of the Silurian Period, with sea-lilies, corals and other life-forms.

CHAPTER 6
FISHES AND FERNS

We do not know a great deal about the Earth before the spread of life, at the beginning of the Cambrian Period, but there is one thing about which we are sure: the climates were not always the same. There have been Ice Ages now and then all through the Earth's history. The last of them ended only 10,000 years ago, but there have been others, and there was certainly one in the Pre-Cambrian Era.

Many ideas have been put forward to explain the Ice Ages. They may have been due to very slight changes in the Earth's path round the Sun, or in the tilt of the axis, which has not always been the same as it is now ($23\frac{1}{2}$ degrees). It is also possible that the cold periods have been caused by changes in the amount of heat sent to us by the Sun. At any rate, they have happened, and no doubt they will happen again in the future.

As we have seen, the land-masses are made up of 'plates' which drift slowly around on top of the mantle. When one large land-mass collides with another, it will push up ranges of mountains; later, these mountains will be worn away by the action of wind and water (a process which we call erosion), after which new ranges will be formed. The first land-masses drifted around in this way, so that during the early part of the Earth's story the map was quite unlike that of today. Then the lands collected together to make one huge continent, which we call Pangea. Around 200 million years ago Pangea broke up, and its various parts drifted around to make the map we know today.

I will have more to say about this later. Meanwhile, let us look back to the Cambrian Period, when there was no life except in the sea. Of special interest were creatures called trilobites, which looked rather like beetles

The Earth flattened out to show how the super-continent of Pangea was made up of today's more familiar continents.

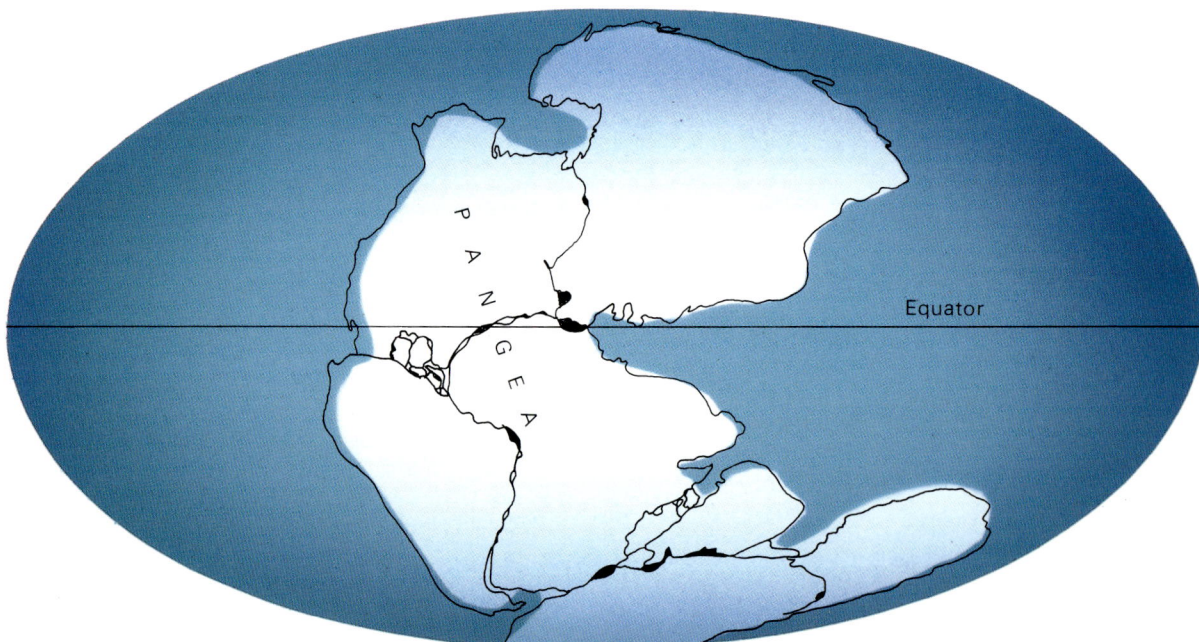

P A N G E A

Equator

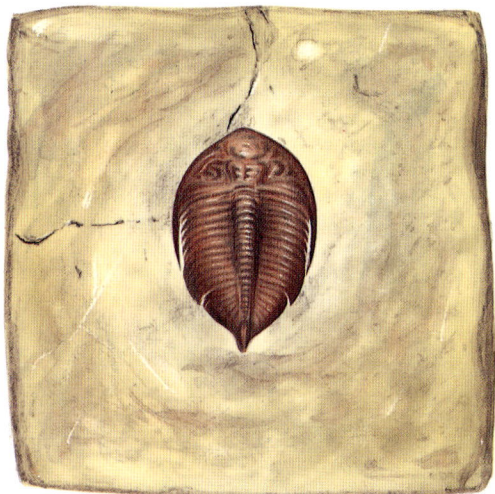

A trilobite fossil in limestone.

with shells, and were up to 25 inches (60 centimetres) long. They had spines, and many legs; they spent most of their time crawling about on the sea-bottoms. During the Cambrian Period they were the commonest life-forms in the world, and they did not disappear until about 250 million years ago. No trilobites exist today; we know them only from their fossils.

Slowly, sea life became more widespread. Fishes appeared during the next period, the Ordovician, but the lands were still lifeless, and there was a long Ice Age. Plants first spread on to the lands during the Silurian Period, and this meant a change in the Earth's air.

Our air contains a great deal of oxygen, and it is this gas which we use for breathing. We take in oxygen, and breathe out the heavier gas carbon dioxide (the gas which makes soft drinks fizzy). The early atmosphere contained so much carbon dioxide that it would have been of no use to us. However, plants 'breathe in' carbon dioxide and give off oxygen, so that as soon as they had spread across the lands they altered the make-up of the air. Of course this did not happen quickly, but over hundreds of millions of years most of the original carbon dioxide was replaced by free oxygen.

The rocks formed during the next geological period are red; you can see them if you go to Devon in the West of England, which is why the period is known as the Devonian. Fishes became very common in the seas, and the lands were covered with tall ferns. Now, too, we come to early insects, and also amphibians – that is to say, creatures which can live either in the sea or on dry land. The frogs and toads of today come down directly from the amphibians which lived in the Devonian fern-forests of four hundred million years ago.

The red sandstone cliffs at Caldey Island were formed during the Devonian Period.

CHAPTER 7
THE COAL FORESTS

Coal is made up of the element carbon. Much of the coal we now use was laid down between 360 and 286 million years ago, and so this geological period is called the Carboniferous.

The arrangement of lands and seas was still changing as the great plates drifted around. At this time there was one large land-mass which we call Gondwana, made up of what is now South America, Africa, India, Australia and Antarctica joined together. Gondwana moved slowly toward another large land-mass, Laurasia, made up of what is now North America together with Europe. The two collided, forcing up great ranges of moutains, and linked up to make the super-continent of Pangea.

By now there were swarms of fishes in the seas, some of which were the forerunners of our present-day sharks. Teeth from these old sharks have been found as fossil remains in the rocks of the time – chiefly rocks which we call

Giant dragonflies dominated the fern-forests in the Carboniferous Period.

The position of the Earth's plates during the Carboniferous Period.

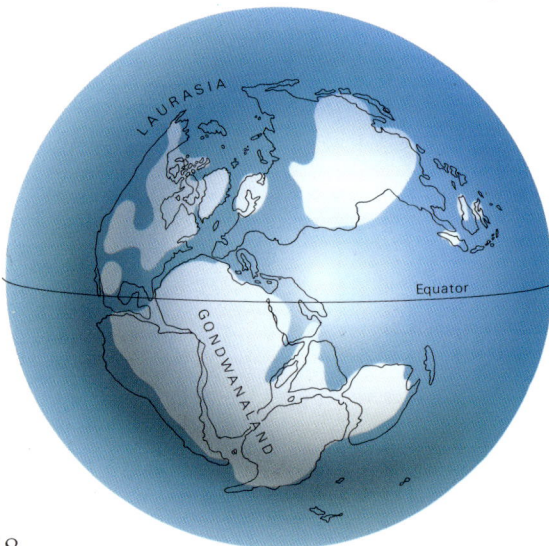

limestone, made up of the remains of tiny shells packed together. But it was on land that life was developing at the greatest rate. Amphibians were spreading, even though most of them were small. There were insects of many kinds, including great dragonflies whose wings stretched out to at least two feet. These dragonflies were the largest insects which have ever lived on the Earth.

There were forests during the Carboniferous Period, but there were no trees; the forests were made up of ferns, club-mosses and horsetails. For millions of years the world was warm, and there were many shallow seas, so that the amphibians were able to live around the coasts.

Along the edges of the seas, rivers dropped material brought down from the hills. Swamps were formed, upon which grew the ferns, club-mosses and horsetails, some of which reached

heights of hundreds of feet. When they died and fell down, they formed thick layers of peat, and when these peat layers were buried underneath new material they turned into coal. It is this coal which we are digging up and burning today.

The coal-forest world must have been

Trees and other plants in the Carboniferous coal-forest decayed to form peat.

a strange place; we can easily picture the huge dragonflies flying around in the fern-forests. As yet there were no dangerous land creatures, but a change was coming. A new Ice Age began toward the end of the Carboniferous Period. It lasted until well into the next period, the Permian, and many types of creatures died out. By the end of the Permian, for example, there were no trilobites left.

The first reptiles had appeared – the creatures from which our snakes are descended. At first they were small, some of them like tiny crocodiles, but before long they spread all over the lands. The map was altering, too. The super-continent of Pangea was almost complete, and all the main land-masses of the world were joined together.

The long Ice Age ended in the middle of the Permian Period, and the world warmed up once more. The cold spell had wiped out many types of creatures, but as soon as it was over the reptiles were able to develop. We were coming to the age of dinosaurs, the largest and most fearsome creatures which the world has ever known.

CHAPTER 8
THE DINOSAURS

Go to any good natural history museum, and you will see dinosaurs – not the real creatures, the last of which died at least 65 million years ago, but very clever models of them. We have found complete fossil skeletons of the dinosaurs, so that we know exactly how they looked.

They were, of course, reptiles, and had developed from the small crocodile-like creatures of the Permian. They lived on the Earth for 140 million years, all through the era which we call the Mesozoic and which is divided into three periods: Triassic, Jurassic and Cretaceous. (I am sorry about these strange names, but, as I have said, it is best to become used to them at once.) The first true dinosaurs appeared in the late Triassic, just over 200 million years ago, at about the time that the super-continent of Pangea began to break up. During the rest of the Mesozoic Era, they ruled the world.

They were of many kinds. The largest of all, the tyrannosaurus, towered to at least 20 feet (over 6 metres), and walked on its two hind legs, because its front legs were much too short. It had long, sharp teeth, and must have been able to kill almost every other kind of creature. There were some dinosaurs with huge claws, used to tear their victims apart, and others which were covered with 'bony' plates. Not all the dinosaurs were flesh-eaters, however; some were small and harmless.

Some dinosaurs could fly, or at least glide from one 'tree' to another; these were the pterodactyls, which appeared around 150 million years ago. Pterodactyls were reptiles, not birds, but we are not so sure about the archæopteryx, which had a skeleton like that of a dinosaur but feathers like those of a bird. Certainly there has been a recent discovery, in China, of a fossil which is certainly like that of a true bird, about the size of a present-day sparrow.

There were dinosaurs in the seas, too, some of them just as terrifying as those on the lands. No part of the world was safe from them. Yet quite suddenly, at the end of the Mesozoic Era, the dinosaurs disappeared.

Why did this happen? We have to

Were the dinosaurs wiped out 65 million years ago by climate changes after a collision between the Earth and an asteroid?

A massive diplodocus skeleton in the Natural History Museum in London.

admit that we do not know. The dinosaurs had very small brains, and were less intelligent than a modern kitten, but there were no other living creatures which could destroy them. Changes in the climate may have been the cause; if the world became much hotter or much cooler, the dinosaurs would not have been able to alter their way of life. But there is another idea which has met with great support. The dinosaurs could have been wiped out as the result of a collision between the Earth and an asteroid.

Asteroids, or minor planets, are small bodies, most of which move round the Sun between the orbits of Mars and Jupiter – much further away from the Sun than we are. However, there are some asteroids which can move inward, and pass close by us. If the Earth were hit by an asteroid a few miles in diameter, the damage would be tremendous. A huge crater would be formed, and there would be violent volcanic eruptions. Dust flung upward would cause a 'cloud' which might last for hundreds of years, so that no sunlight could reach the ground. Many plants would die, and the dinosaurs would quickly run short of food. They would have little hope of living in a world which had become suddenly cold and dark.

This may or may not be true, but it is certain that by the end of the Cretaceous Period, 65 million years ago, the dinosaurs were dead. The Earth was becoming a very different sort of place.

CHAPTER 9
THE NEW WORLD

The death of the dinosaurs marked a turning-point in the Earth's history. The mammals, from which we are descended, were able to live in peace in the forests and plains where the dinosaurs had once wandered. Also, the break-up of Pangea was followed by a slow drifting-apart of the land-masses, so that the map of the world became more and more like that of today.

Mammals are warm-blooded, unlike reptiles, and they have much larger brains. During the 40 million years following the end of the dinosaurs, the early mammals began to change into animals of the kind we can just about recognize. Some of them were the ancestors of our elephants, dogs and cats, while a small animal known as an eohippus is quite clearly an early kind of horse. There was also the arsinotherium, which had two small horns above its eyes and another enormous horn pointing forward above its nose. It is obvious that the arsinotherium was the ancestor of our present-day rhinoceros.

Of special interest were the primates, which lived in trees and became widespread as soon as the dinosaurs were out of the way. There can be no doubt that these small creatures were our own ancestors. It is not true to say that men are descended from monkeys, but it is quite true that both men and monkeys come down from the tree-living primates of the Eocene Period, more than fifty million years ago.

For many millions of years the world was warmer than it is now. Grasslands spread over the continents, and animals became used to living in the open rather than in forests. By the end of the Miocene Period, about five million years ago, there were animals which we could easily recognize today, and the world was starting to look really 'modern'. There were pigs, elephants, deer, dogs, cats, and birds of the kind we know now, though there were also animals which have died out – such as the mammoth, the mastodon, the cave bear and the sabre-toothed tiger.

During the Pliocene Period, between five and two million years ago, came the most important development of all. The first men appeared.

The Eohippus (*below*) from the Eocene Period and the Mesohippus (*right*) from the Miocene Period are obviously ancestors of the horse.

The Woolly Mammoth only died out after the last Great Ice Age.

It did not happen suddenly, and it is not easy to tell from the fossil remains just which creatures can be classed as 'men' and which cannot. For example, there were the so-called Southern Apes, whose fossils have been found in Africa, and who lived around 5 million years ago. They walked very much as we do, but they were small – no more than four feet in height – and their brains were no larger than those of monkeys. Yet on the whole, it seems that they were more man-like than ape-like.

The last of the Southern Apes died about a million years ago, but well before that a new kind of man-like creature had appeared. The fossils which we have found show us that the newcomers were definitely human, but they could not speak in the way that we do. Their language must have been made up of grunts!

Next came the Neanderthal men, who date back about 300,000 years. They were unlike us in appearance, and seem to have been unable to talk. The last of them died out around 30,000 years ago, and were followed by the Cro-Magnon men, who were much more like you and me, and who could certainly speak. They knew how to make fire, they made stone tools, and they buried their dead. But they had to live in an unfriendly world; the Earth was in the grip of a new Ice Age.

CHAPTER 10
THE GREAT ICE AGE

Most people have heard about the Ice Age. It was not simply one long, unbroken spell lasting for tens of thousands of years, but during the Pleistocene Period, which began two million years ago and ended only 10,000 years ago, there were several cold spells which had a great effect upon all living things.

What we usually call the Great Ice Age was made up of several parts. The first cold spell began 120,000 years ago, and was at its worst 70,000 years ago, after which the world became warmer again; we had come to what is called an 'interglacial'. Then the coldness returned, and was again at its worst about 18,000 years ago, when the ice covered many of the continents. By now the drifting plates had made the world map very much like that of today, though

Britain was still joined on to the mainland of Europe; our present North Sea was dry. There was also a land bridge between Alaska in North America and Siberia in Asia. It was only when the ice melted that the low-lying lands were flooded, so that Britain was at last separated from Europe.

During the coldest part of the Ice Age, all of Scotland and much of England was covered; the ice-sheet ended just north of where London now stands. In America, the limit of the ice cut across the middle of the United States. But then the world warmed up once more, so that by 10,000 years ago the main Ice Age was over. Today the only parts of the world which are still permanently frozen are those near the poles.

For part of the Ice Age, both Neanderthalers and Cro-Magnon men lived on the Earth. Whether they fought each other, so that in the end the

During the Great
Ice Age the ice-sheets
covered much more
of the Earth's surface
than they do now.

Cro-Magnon man was a hunter-gatherer who still lived in caves, but had discovered fire.

drew on the walls. We have also found small models of men, women and animals. Stone was widely used to make tools and weapons, because although it is hard it can easily be chipped into any shape needed. One particular kind of stone – flint – was used to make hand axes, which could be used to skin animals. This is why the period which ended 10,000 years ago is usually called the Old Stone Age.

The first villages were built at about the time that the ice began to melt. During the Middle Stone Age, people began to use bows and arrows for hunting and in war. They also built boats; and as time went by, human beings travelled all over the world.

Even since the end of the Great Ice Age there have been definite changes in the climate, with warmer and cooler periods. We cannot be sure that the Ice Age is finally over. As we have seen, there were 'interglacials' between the cold spells, and it is quite possible that in the future the ice-sheets will grow once more.

Yet there is another point to bear in mind. During the past hundred years or so we have been adding to the amount of carbon dioxide in the air, because of our factories and industries. Carbon dioxide acts in the same way as a greenhouse, shutting in the Sun's heat, and it has been suggested that the extra amount of carbon dioxide is making the whole world hotter. If this is so, then the ice will start to melt, the sea-level will rise, and parts of the lands will be flooded. Whether or not this is really happening we do not yet know; but if we find out that we really are changing the Earth's climate, we must make sure that we change our way of life before we do real harm.

Neanderthalers were wiped out, we do not know, but by the time of the last great cold spell only the Cro-Magnons were left. These people of the Ice Age were hunters, and lived by capturing and eating animals such as mammoth and reindeer. The animal skins were used to make clothes; fat was used for oil lamps, and bones were made into tools.

Cro-Magnon men built huts, though many of them lived in caves, where we can still see the coloured pictures of animals and hunting scenes that they

CHAPTER 11
MAPPING THE EARTH

We have now been able to map the whole of the Earth. Even the polar lands have been explored, and we may be sure that there are no 'lost worlds' waiting to be discovered. Much of the work has been carried out by cameras carried in man-made moons or artificial satellites, which are launched by rockets and put into closed paths round the Earth. Many hundreds of these satellites have been sent up since October 1957, when the Russians launched the first of them – *Sputnik 1*, about the size of a football*.

To fix your position on the Earth's surface you need to know two things: your latitude, and your longitude. To explain what is meant, I must say a little about *angles*.

A full circle is divided into 360 degrees, as shown in the first diagram. This means that a right angle is divided into 90 degrees. The latitude of any particular place is simply the angular distance from the Earth's equator, in degrees, as measured from the centre of the globe (second diagram). London, for example, is 51 degrees north of the equator, while Sydney in Australia is 34 degrees south. It is clear from the diagram that the latitude of the equator is 0 degrees, while the north pole is at 90 degrees north and the south pole at 90 degrees south.

This is straightforward enough, because we can start at the Earth's equator, which – as we have seen – cuts the world in half. But we also need our

*I have described this in the second-book in this series, Space Travel for the Under Tens.

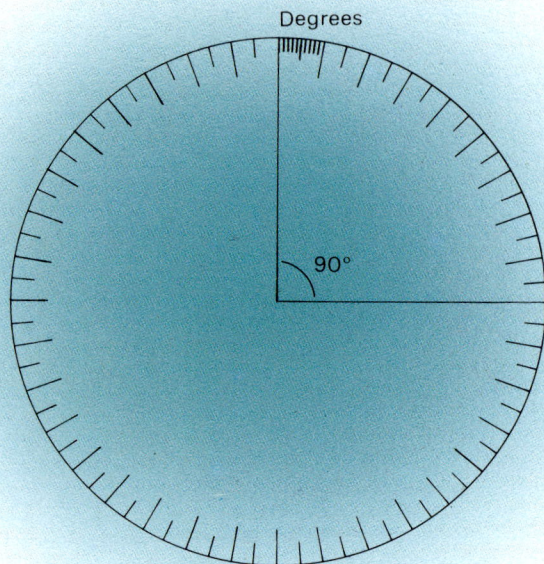

A quarter of a circle is 90 degrees and a whole circle is 360 degrees.

longitude, and this is rather less simple.

If you take an orange, you can make a shallow cut right round it to divide it into two equal parts; this may be called the 'equator' of the orange. Now cut a second line, passing through both the top and bottom of the orange and again dividing it into two parts, making the new line at right angles to the 'equator' (see diagram). On the Earth, a line of this kind is called a *meridian*, and will pass through both poles.

We need one special meridian to act as a starting-point, and in 1884 it was agreed that this starting-point should be the meridian which passes through the Royal Greenwich Observatory, in Outer London. This is taken as longitude 0 degrees, and divides the world into two hemispheres: eastern and western. Longitude, then, is the angular distance of any place east or west of the Greenwich meridian. For examples, Cardiff in Wales has longitude 3 degrees west, while Sydney is at 151 degrees east. The opposite side of

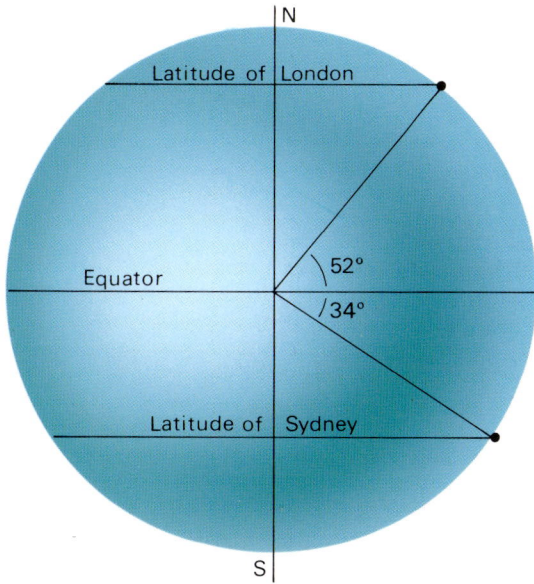

The latitude of anywhere on the Earth can be found by measuring its angular distance from the equator.

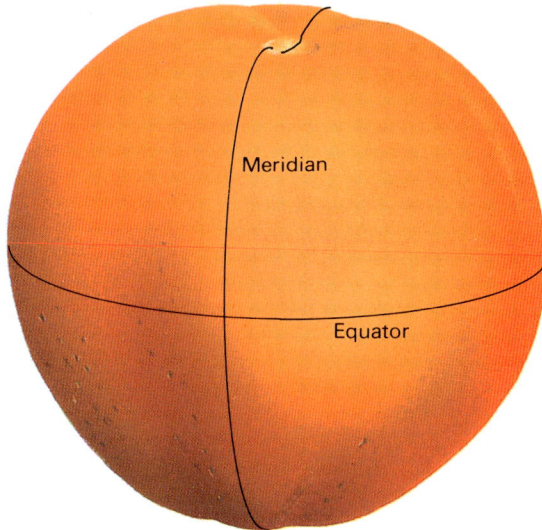

An orange cut to show the equator and a meridian.

the Greenwich meridian – longitude 180 degrees – runs through the South Seas close to New Zealand.

We have seen that the Earth's axis is tilted at an angle of $23\frac{1}{2}$ degrees. The parts of the Earth between latitudes $23\frac{1}{2}$ degrees north and south make up what is called the tropical zone; from here, there are times when the Sun passes straight over head, so that it casts no shadows at all. The regions within $23\frac{1}{2}$ degrees of the poles are called the Arctic Zone (in the north) and the Antarctic Zone (in the south). From here there are days when the Sun never rises, or when it never sets. Go to a latitude greater than $66\frac{1}{2}$ degrees north or south, and during part of the summer you will be able to see the Sun at 'midnight'. Lerwick, in the Shetland Isles, has a latitude of just over 60 degrees north, so that from there you cannot see the midnight sun – but during summer-time it is quite easy to read a newspaper at midnight without using a torch!

CHAPTER 12
INSIDE THE EARTH

It is not easy to find out just what the Earth is like inside. Remember, the world is nearly 8000 miles (over 12,800 kilometres) in diameter, and even our deepest mines go down to no more than $2\frac{1}{4}$ miles ($3\frac{1}{2}$ kilometres). Nobody has ever dug through to the Earth's core – and nobody ever will.

The surface upon which we live is the top of what geologists call the crust. More than half of it is covered with water, and some of the oceans are very deep. If you could take the world's highest mountain, Everest, and put its base on the bottom of the deepest part of the Pacific Ocean, not even the top of the mountain would poke out.

The crust is not the same thickness everywhere. It is about 4 miles (7 kilometres) deep below the oceans, but on average about 25 miles (40 kilometres) below the continents, and below the world's highest peaks, those of the Himalayas, the crust may go down to as much as 56 miles (90 kilometres). As you go down into the crust, the temperature rises. At the bottom of the world's deepest mine, in South Africa, the rock temperature is 131 degrees Fahrenheit (55 degrees Centigrade).

At the bottom of the crust there is a sudden change. We come to the sticky, outer mantle, where the rocks are so hot that they are no longer solid; they can flow, rather in the manner of treacle. The boundary between the crust and the mantle is known as the Moho, because it was first discovered by a Jugoslav scientist with the tongue-twisting name of Andrija Mohorovičić.

More than thirty years ago there was a plan to bore a hole right through the Earth's crust, to see what the top of the mantle was like. This plan became known, rather naturally, as Project Mohole. A small test hole was sunk off the coast of California, but it soon became clear that the cost would be

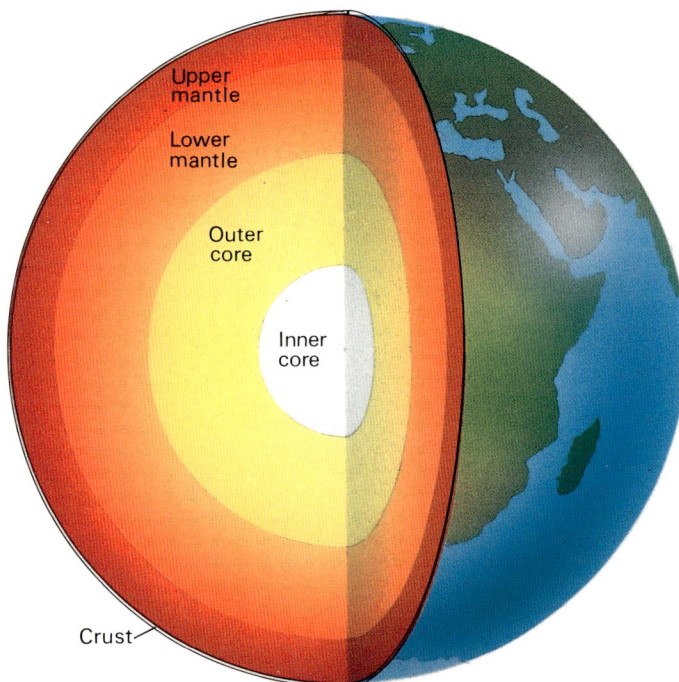

Upper mantle

Lower mantle

Outer core

Inner core

Crust

The internal structure of the Earth, showing the solid inner core, the liquid metal outer core, the molten rock of the lower and upper mantle, and the very thin crust.

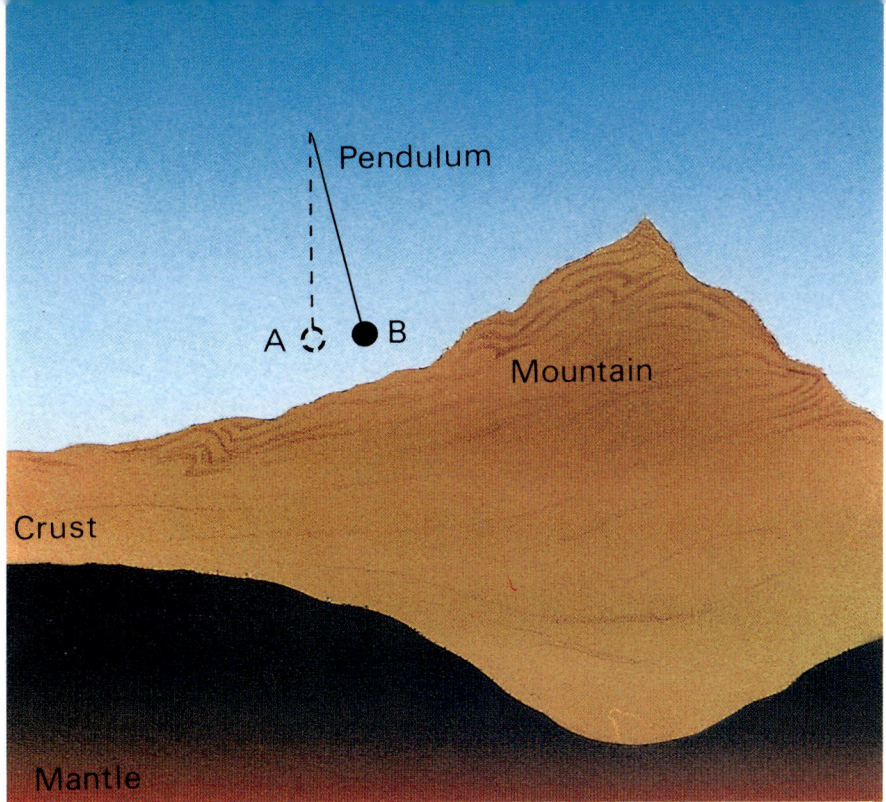

Instead of hanging straight down, a pendulum will be pulled towards a mountain because of the effect of gravity.

much greater than had been expected – at least 125 million dollars – and nobody was at all sure just what would be learned from making the hole, so that in 1966 the whole scheme was given up.

Below the mantle we come to the Earth's core, which is divided into two main parts. The inner part is over 1250 miles (2000 kilometres) in diameter. It is made up chiefly of iron and nickel, and is so 'squeezed' that it is solid. Nobody is sure of the exact temperature, but it is probably about 5000 degrees Centigrade, not much less than that at the surface of the Sun. Round the solid core comes a thick layer of liquid metal, 1400 miles (2300 kilometres) deep, again made up chiefly of iron and nickel. It is here that the Earth's magnetic field is produced, because, as we have seen, iron is magnetic, and the currents set up as it 'sloshes around' cause a dynamo effect.

In 1774 a very important experiment was carried out in Scotland by a well-known astronomer, Nevil Maskelyne. He set up a pendulum near a high mountain, Schiehallion, as shown in the diagram. The pendulum ought to have hung straight down, but the gravitational pull of the mountain dragged it slightly to one side, and the amount of drag told Maskelyne how massive the mountain was. This in turn gave a good value for the average density of the Earth's crust.

We also need to know the total mass of the Earth. This can be done by measuring the Earth's gravitational pull upon the Moon. It has been found that the mass of the whole of the Earth is 6,000,000,000,000,000,000,000 tons. (If you count up the number of zeros you will find that there are 21 of them!) From this, we can find that the Earth 'weighs' five and a half times as much as a globe of the same size would do if it were made up entirely of water, so that the central core is very dense indeed as well as being very hot.

CHAPTER 13
EARTHQUAKES

I have already said something about the way in which the Earth's crust is divided into slabs or 'plates', which drift around on top of the fluid mantle. The speeds of the plates are very slow – only a few centimetres per year – but over a sufficiently long time this is enough to change the world map completely.

Molten rock, known as magma, can be pushed up through cracks in the sea-bottoms. This 'sea-floor spreading', as it is called, pushes the continents around. There are great ranges of mountains which lie almost or fully below sea-level; one of these is the Mid-Atlantic Ridge, which pokes out in a few places – Iceland, for example, is simply the top of an undersea mountain. Material is being pushed out through the Ridge, and is forcing Africa and South America apart at the rate of just over 1 inch (roughly 3 cm) per year. In other places one plate is pushing its way underneath another, so that it becomes hotter and melts back into the mantle.

In places where two plates are meeting, and are pushing against each other, there is always a danger that the strain will build up enough to produce a sudden 'snap' or shock. This is the cause of an earthquake.

Earthquakes can do a tremendous amount of damage. One of the worst shocks of modern times struck Tokyo, the capital of Japan, on 1 September 1923. Houses collapsed; great fires broke out, and could not be put out because all the water pipes had been broken, and most of the city was ruined, with the loss of over 100,000 lives. Even worse was the Chinese earthquake of 1976, when at least 600,000 people were

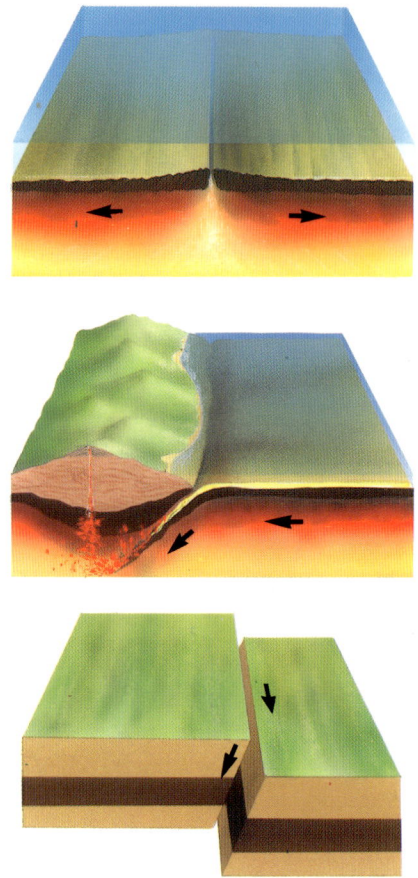

The three types of fault line: a) sea-floor spreading where two plates are drifting apart, b) an induction fault where one plate is being forced underneath the other, and c) a strike-slip fault where two plates are sliding alongside each other.

killed. There have been violent earthquakes in Europe, too, though Britain is more or less free of them, and only a few mild shocks have been felt here.

We cannot tell just when earthquakes will happen, but we do know the danger-zones. These are mainly places where the crustal plates are either moving together or are sliding alongside one another. One such area is along what is known as the San Andreas Fault, which passes through California. There was a major earthquake in San Francisco in 1906, and another in 1986. It is very likely that there will be another San Francisco earthquake within the next few years, but all we can really do is to make buildings in these parts of the world as strong as possible.

Earthquakes set up 'waves' in the body of the Earth. These waves are of several kinds. First there are the P-waves, which we can call 'push-waves'. The best way to explain these is to picture a railway engine bumping into a line of trucks; the first truck bumps the second, the second truck bumps the third, and so on all the way down the line. To make the picture more correct, we must suppose that after being hit the trucks bounce back to their original positions, jerking to and fro for some time afterwards.

Next there are the S-waves, or shake-waves, which are like the waves set up in a mat when you shake it by one end. The S-waves move more slowly than the P-waves (about $2\frac{3}{4}$ miles ($4\frac{1}{2}$ kilometres) per second, as against 5 miles (8 kilometres) per second). There are also the L or long waves, which travel round the Earth's surface at about $2\frac{1}{2}$ miles (4 kilometres) per second, and cause most of the damage.

These waves can tell us a great deal about the make-up of the Earth itself. Waves move fastest through dense material, and, as we know, the Earth becomes denser as we move down – so by measuring the speeds of the P and S waves at different levels, we can measure the densities at various depths below the Earth's surface. The rule is, 'The denser, the faster'. We also know that S-waves cannot pass through liquid, and so they are blocked by the liquid part of the Earth's core, while the P-waves can travel straight through. This tells us how large the liquid part of the core must be.

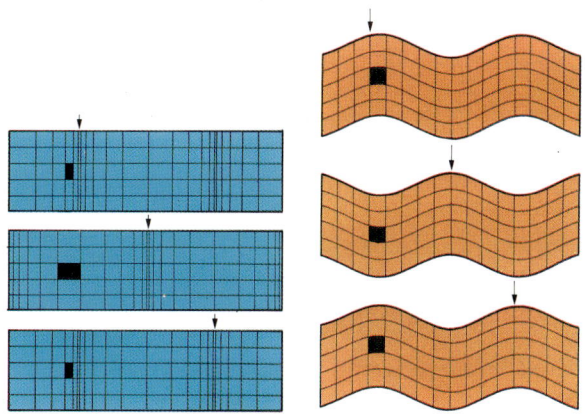

P-waves travel quickly through solids or liquids, but S-waves can only pass slowly through solids.

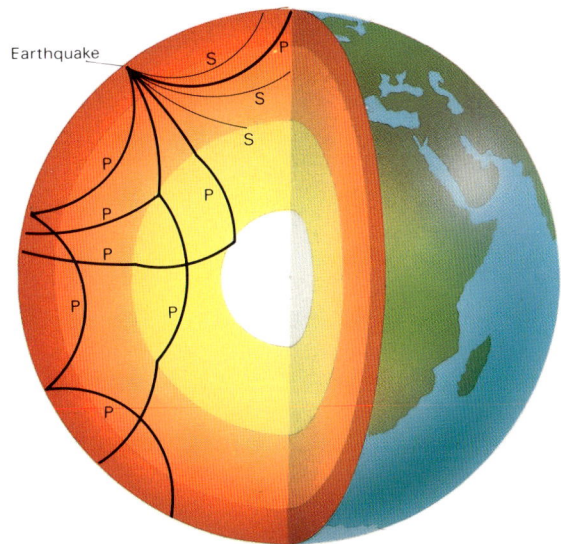

P-waves can travel through the liquid part of the Earth's core but the S-waves cannot.

The first earthquake-recorder or 'seismometer' was made by a Chinese, Chang Heng, in the second century AD. It was made up of an upside-down copper dome, very carefully balanced. Round the rim were eight dragons' heads, each with a small copper ball on its tongue, and below each dragon was a bronze frog with its mouth wide open. As soon as the instrument was jolted by an earthquake, the ball closest to the direction of the earthquake wave was shot out of the dragon's mouth into the jaws of the frog below!

CHAPTER 14
VOLCANOES

A volcano in eruption is a wonderful sight, with red-hot lava pouring out from below the ground and fountains of fire shooting into the sky. Yet volcanoes have killed many people over the years, and there have been some terrible disasters. One of the worst took place in AD 79, when Mount Vesuvius, in Italy, destroyed the city of Pompeii – quite without warning, because the volcano had not erupted for so long that it had been thought to be dead, or extinct. Pompeii was covered with ash, and its people were choked by poisonous gases, while the nearby city of Herculaneum was swamped by boiling mud. Go to Pompeii now, and you can see what is left of the old buildings.

Vesuvius has erupted many times since then, though never with such violence. When it is 'quiet' there is no danger in climbing it and looking straight down into the crater. It is not the only Italian volcano; others are Stromboli, which is sending out steam and ash for much of the time, and Etna.

Some of the world's most interesting volcanoes are in Hawaii. The two highest are Mauna Kea, which is extinct, and Mauna Loa, which is active. Mauna Kea has become very important to astronomers, because one of our largest observatories has been built on top of it.

Hawaii can tell us a great deal about how volcanoes work. The mantle below the crust is made up of hot, fluid rock or magma. The magma may force its way up through a weak point or 'hot spot' in the crust, so that a volcano is built up; when the magma reaches the surface it cools and solidifies, to become lava.

The domes of the observatory on the extinct volcano of Mauna Kea on Hawaii.

Mauna Kea was built up in this way. Because the plates in the crust are moving slowly around, Mauna Kea has moved away from the 'hot spot' and no longer erupts, while Mauna Loa now stands over the 'hot spot' and is very active indeed. On one occasion lava from Mauna Loa rolled down to the outskirts of the town of Hilo, and many of the roads on the island are regularly flooded with lava, so that they have to be re-built.

Volcanoes are of several types. Those of Hawaii are 'shield volcanoes', and are of tremendous size; they rise from the sea-floor, and Mauna Kea and Mauna Loa are actually larger than Everest (which is not a volcano, but an ordinary mountain).

Other volcanoes, such as Vesuvius, are cone-shaped. The magma pushes its way up through a vent or tunnel in the crust; if this vent becomes blocked, the pressure may build up until there is a violent explosion – as happened in AD 79. Much more recently, in 1980, the volcano of Mount St Helens, in the American state of Washington, blew its top away, sending smoke and ash up to a height of 20,000 feet (6000 metres).

There are also volcanoes which are not mountains, but 'fissures', or long cracks in the Earth's crust from which magma pours out. In 1783 one of these fissure volcanoes, Laki, laid waste a large part of Iceland. A fiery river streamed into a lake, turning the water into steam and boiling mud. It was two years before the eruption was over.

There have been even greater eruptions in the past. In about 1500 BC Santorini, an island in the Mediterranean, blew up and caused great ocean waves which flooded parts of the island of Crete. There was an explosion of the same kind in 1883, this time at Krakatoa in the East Indies, when a huge 'wall of water' swept across to Java and Sumatra, washing away three hundred villages and drowning 35,000 people. A new island, built from volcanic material, has now appeared at Krakatoa, but nobody lives there; it must be one of the most dangerous places in the world.

Paricutín, in Mexico, is a 'new' volcano. On 20 February 1943 a farmer was ploughing his cornfield when he saw a crack appear in the ground. Smoke began to pour out, followed by sparks which set nearby trees alight; next

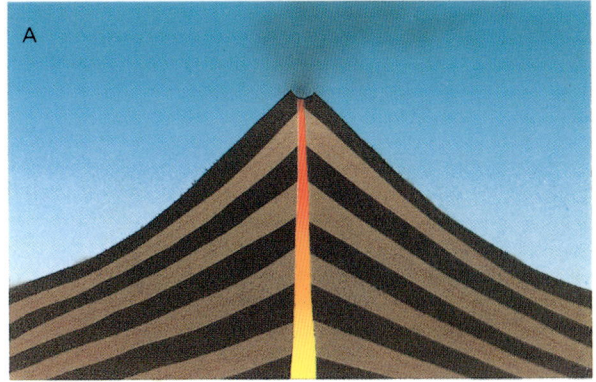

A is a cone-chaped strato volcano like Vesuvius and B is a shield volcano like Mauna Loa.

came red-hot lava, with burning clouds. After only a month a volcano over a thousand feet high towered over the cornfield. By the time that the eruptions ceased, nine years later, the whole area had been ruined and blackened.

Luckily for us, Britain is as free from active volcanoes as it is from powerful earthquakes. We live on a very firm, solid part of the Earth's crust.

Mount Batur in Bali is an active strato volcano. The tip of its cone collapsed after the massive eruption of 1963.

CHAPTER 15
THE OCEAN TIDES

Everyone knows about the tides, and most people know that they are caused mainly by the gravitational pull of the Moon, but things are not so straightforward as might be thought. To explain just what happens, let me start by supposing that the Moon is standing still, and that the Earth is covered by a shallow ocean all round the globe, as in the first diagram.

The Moon is pulling on both the Earth's solid globe and on the water, but the water is the more easily moved, so that it heaps up underneath the Moon and produces a high tide at point A. There is another high tide on the far side of the Earth, at position B, because here the water is being 'left behind', so to speak; it is further away from the Moon, and the pull on it is less.

The Earth spins round once in 24 hours, but the two tidal bulges do not spin with it. Instead, they keep underneath the Moon, and the result is that

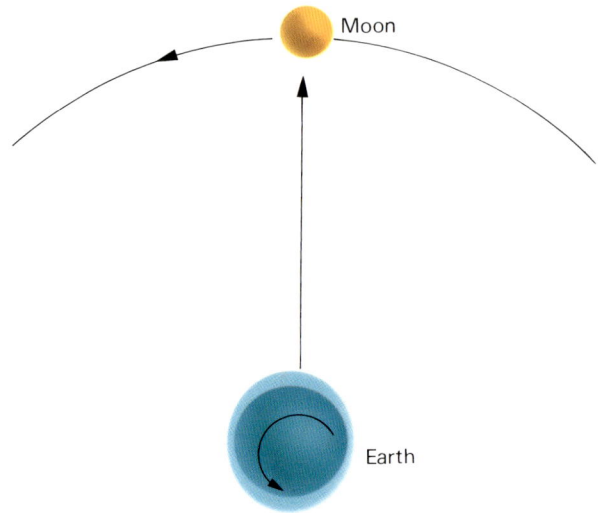

The Moon's gravity is the main cause of our tides.

the bulges seem to sweep round the Earth, giving each place two high tides and two low tides in each 24-hour period.

Of course, the real situation is much less simple. The Earth is not completely water-covered, and the shapes of the lands and seas make the tides much less regular than would otherwise be the case.

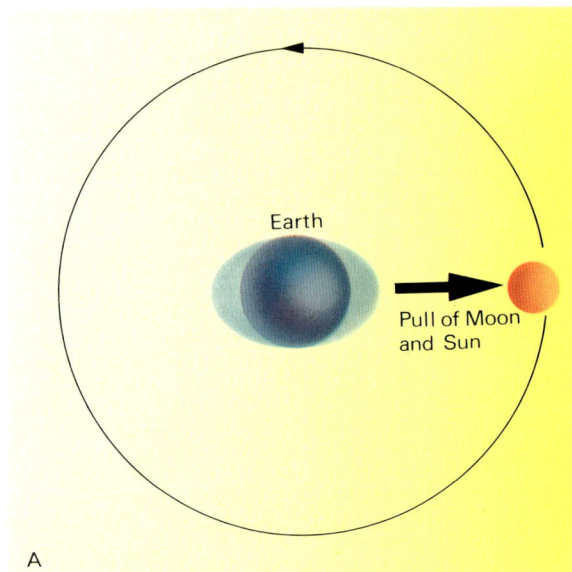

Very high Spring tides occur when the Sun and Moon are pulling in the same direction,

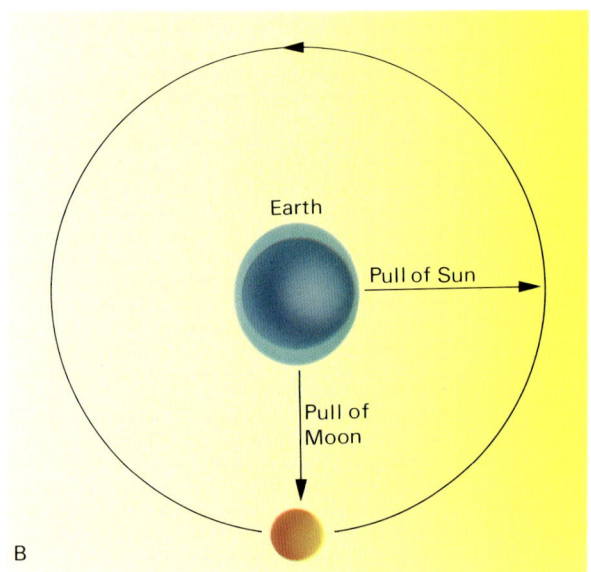

and lower Neap tides when the Sun and Moon are pulling from different directions.

34

High and low tides at Tenby.

Neither is the Moon standing still; it is moving round the Earth in a period of just over 27 days. Also, it takes time for the water to heap up, so that the tidal bulges are not straight underneath the Moon. Different places have tides of different strength; in the Bay of Fundy, on the Canadian coast, there is a difference of about 50 feet (over 14 metres) between high and low tide, while in the shallow Mediterranean the range is no more than about three feet (about one metre).

The Sun also causes tides, but they are much weaker than those of the Moon, because the Sun is 400 times further away. When the Sun and the Moon are 'helping' each other, as in the next diagram, the tides are strong; these are called spring tides (rather a misleading name, because it has nothing to do with the season of spring). When the Sun and the Moon are pulling at right angles to each other, as in the second diagram, we have weaker or 'neap' tides. I will have more to say about the Moon in Chapter 19, but it is worth remembering that we have spring tides when the Moon is new or full, and neap tides when the Moon shows up as a half in our sky.

One effect of the tides is that the Earth's rate of spin is slowing down; the days are becoming longer. This is because of the friction of the water against the sea-bed. The effect is very slight, and the increase in the length of the day is no more than a fraction of a second per century, but it is true that in very ancient times, long before men appeared on Earth, the days were much shorter than they are now.

There are land tides, too, but they are not easy to notice, simply because the land is much more 'solid' than water, and is not so easy to pull up or down.

CHAPTER 16

THE EARTH'S AIR

If you go up in a jet aircraft to a height of thousands of feet, you will have to stay inside a cabin which is air-tight and also kept warm. The air outside is bitterly cold, and also much too thin to be breathed. You may also notice that the sky looks darker blue than it does from ground level. The blueness is caused by the fact that the air particles scatter the blue part of the light coming to us from the Sun; when you are flying at, say, 30,000 feet there is much less air above you, and so the scattering is less.

Even before aircraft had been invented, it was known that the air becomes thinner and cooler with increasing height. Mountaineers have to wear breathing masks when climbing to the tops of very high peaks – such as Everest, which rises to about 5 miles (8 kilometres).

As we have seen, the Earth lost its first atmosphere, because the hydrogen was blown away by the Sun. Our present-day air is made up chiefly of two gases, nitrogen and oxygen; these are heavier than hydrogen, and so the Earth pulls strongly enough to hold them down, and they cannot escape into space.

The bottom layer of the atmosphere, in which we live and in which we find all our 'weather', is known as the troposphere. It stretches upward for about 7 miles (11 kilometres), so that it covers the tops of even our highest mountains. Above it comes the stratosphere, which goes up to a height of about 30 miles (50 kilometres). The stratosphere contains a layer of ozone, which is a special form of oxygen, and which protects us from dangerous radiations coming from space. There have

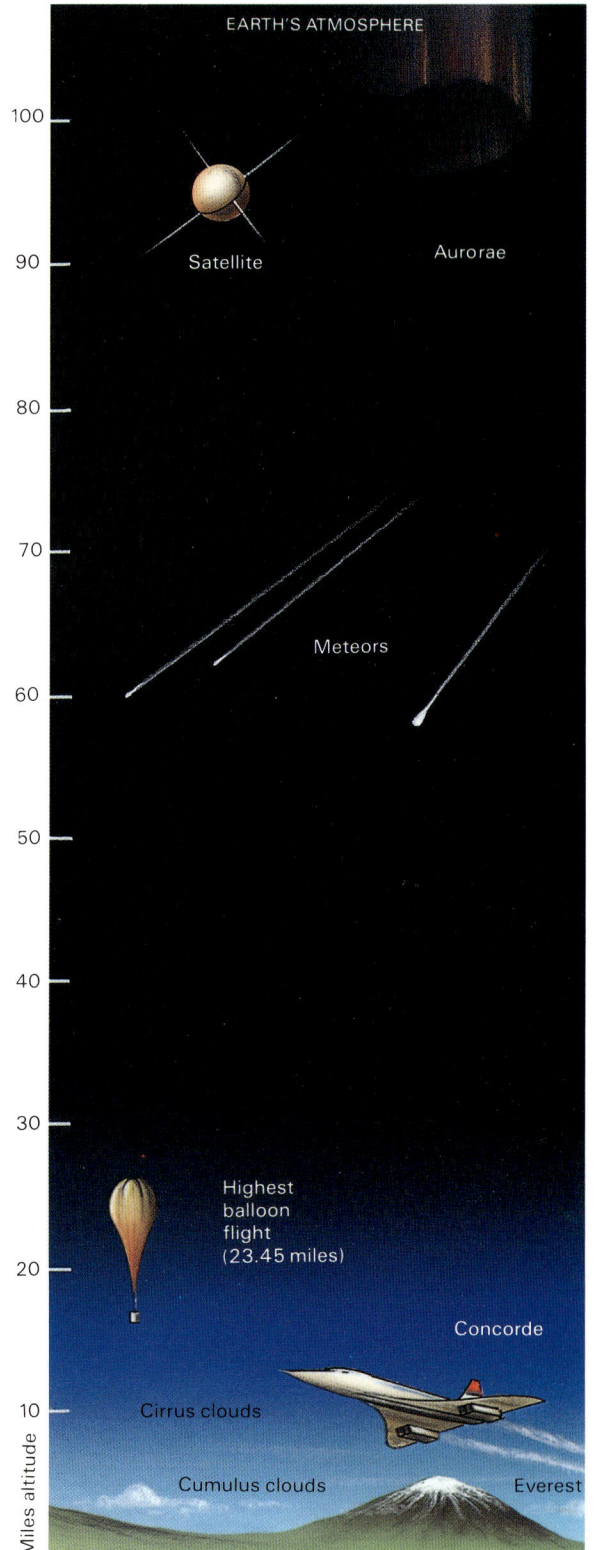

A cross-section through the Earth's atmosphere.

This NASA astronaut has to wear a space suit because there is no air to breathe at this height above the Earth and it is also very cold. Also there is no air pressure.

been fears that some of the chemicals we use today may be damaging the ozone layer, and if this proves to be true we will have to stop using these chemicals before they can do any more harm.

Higher up still we come to the ionosphere, where there are layers of *ions*, electrically-charged atom-groups of oxygen and nitrogen, which make long-distance radio communication possible. Radio waves travel in straight lines, so that a signal sent out from, say, London would not be expected to curve round the Earth and reach an operator in New York; but some of the radio waves can be reflected by the ionosphere, so that they can reach far-away parts of the world.

There is no sharp upper edge to the atmosphere. It simply goes on thinning out until there is none left, and it is not easy to say just where it 'ends', but

there is not much of it left above a height of about 120 miles (200 kilometres). We know this because of the behaviour of meteors, which are solid particles, usually smaller than grains of sand, which come in from outer space. When they dash into the air, moving at up to 45 miles (72 kilometres) per second, they rub against the air-particles; this makes them hot, and they burn away, producing the bright streaks which we call shooting-stars. By the time that a meteor has dropped down to a height of 40 miles (65 kilometres) it has burned away completely.

The Earth is the only planet in the Solar System to have air of the kind we can breathe. When we go to other worlds, we will have to stay inside our space-ships or our bases, unless we wear special suits and carry tanks of oxygen with us all the time.

CHAPTER 17
WINDS, CLOUDS AND STORMS

The state of the Earth's air is always changing. By now we can usually tell what the weather is going to be like for a day or two ahead, but the forecasters can often make mistakes – as happened in October 1987, when a violent storm hit South England, blowing down thousands of trees and causing widespread damage to buildings. It had certainly not been expected, so that people were not ready for it.

Air is 'heavy', and is pressing down on us all the time. Winds are due to differences in pressure between one place and another, because air blows from a region of high pressure, where it is being 'squashed', to a region where the pressure is less. The greater the pressure difference, the stronger the wind.

There are two main kinds of weather systems. In a 'low', the pressure is least near the centre of the system and rises all round, while in a 'high' the situation is reversed – high in the middle, low all round. Lines joining up places where

A typical weather map of the British Isles showing the air pressure, a weather front, the amount of cloud cover, the wind speed and where it is raining.

The sudden storm of October 1987 was very rare for Southern England, and blew down thousands of large trees.

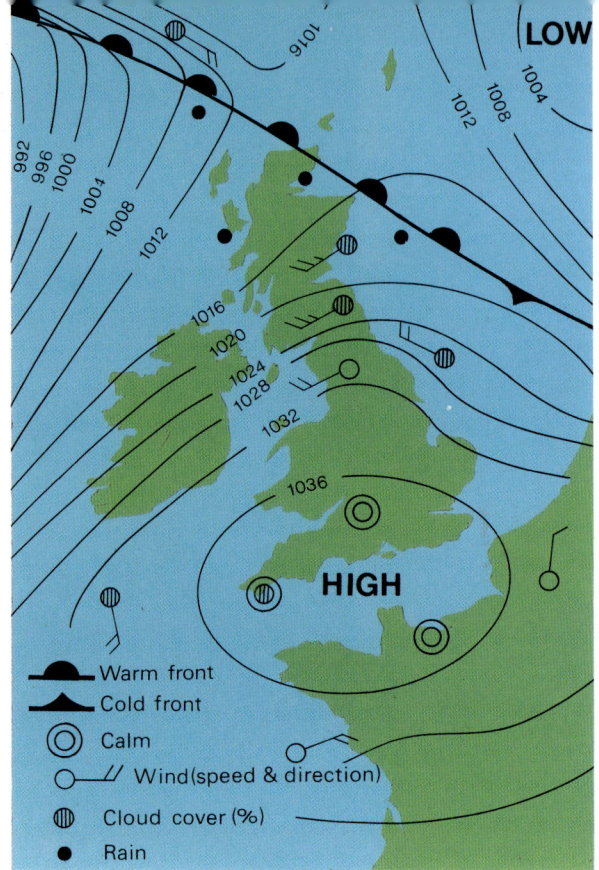

the pressure is the same are called isobars. Look at these isobars next time you see a weather map on your television screen, and note whether they are close together or wide apart. If they are close, then expect strong winds.

Air contains water vapour. Warm air can hold more moisture than cold air, so that if the air is cooled some of the moisture in it will condense to form cloud. (You can see much the same sort of thing in your kitchen. If you boil a kettle, steam will come out of the spout, because the air coming from inside the kettle is suddenly cooled down to the temperature of the air outside.)

If a moving air-mass meets rising ground, such as the slope of a hill, it will be forced upward, cooling down

High cloud (*above*) is an early indication of a warm front. Fluffy clouds (*below*) show the presence of a cold front. This one is massive and could develop into a thunderstorm.

and producing cloud. Clouds will also be formed if warm, moist air moves over colder ground.

If a moving mass of warm air catches up a mass of cold air, it will be forced upward, because it is less dense and cannot 'push' the cold air out of the way. The result is what weather-men call a warm front. The first sign of it is usually the appearance of very high clouds, made up of ice crystals; these gradually thicken up, and then come the main cloud layers, which are likely to produce rain. A cold front is different. This time it is the cold air which catches up the warm air, and forces it up, so that we see large clouds which often look like bunches of cotton-wool in the sky.

Thunderstorms are also found with cold fronts. The thunder-clouds are very large, stretching up so far that their tops are made of ice. They are electrically charged, and a flash of lightning is simply a giant spark between points with different electrical charges – that is to say, between the cloud itself and the Earth's surface. The heat caused by the lightning makes the air expand suddenly, and this is the cause of thunder. Thunder is quite harmless, but lightning is not, and kills many people each year.

Hail is often associated with these clouds. A hailstone is not a stone, but a lump of ice. Layers of water freeze on to it as it is carried up and down inside the cloud, and it finally becomes so heavy that it falls to the ground. Some hailstones have been known to grow as large as golf-balls.

Many parts of the world are in constant danger from storms. For example, the town of Darwin, in Northern Australia, was almost completely destroyed in 1970 when it was hit by a violent wind, and hurricanes are very common in some areas of the United States. In Britain we are usually safe, though the great storms of October 1987 and January 1990 make us realize that even here we are still very much at the mercy of the weather.

Hailstones often fall from thunder-clouds, although they are usually smaller than this.

CHAPTER 18
THE EARTH FROM SPACE

The Space Age began on 4 October 1957, with the launching of Russia's artificial satellite *Sputnik 1*. It carried little apart from a radio transmitter, but it was a tremendous importance, because it showed us that we were at last able to travel beyond the Earth.

Aircraft cannot fly at heights greater than a few miles, because they need to have air around them. Rockets, however, can work very well in space. An artificial satellite is taken up by rocket power and put into a closed path round the Earth. It will not fall down, any more than the real Moon does, because it is moving – and there is nothing to stop it.

Yet this is true only if the satellite stays above the 120-mile (200-kilometre) limit. If it comes lower, it will have to fight its way through the denser part of the air. This will set up friction, and the satellite will burn away, just as a meteor does. This is what happened to the first real American space-station, *Skylab*, which was launched in 1972 and was destroyed in 1979, when it broke up after re-entering the atmosphere and scattered pieces of itself over wide areas of Australia.

We have learned a great deal by looking at the Earth from space. For example, satellite pictures can show us whole weather systems, and tell us how the air-masses are behaving. They can give us detailed maps of the whole of the globe, and they can locate regions which are of special interest to geologists, such as parts of the world where we are likely to find oil. They have also

A gigantic low-pressure system approaching the coastline of Morocco.

told us much more about the Earth's magnetic field.

If you take a bar magnet, cover it with a sheet of paper, put some iron filings on top of the paper and then tap, the filings will arrange themselves in a definite way which marks the lines of magnetic force. Because of the liquid iron moving around in the Earth's core, the Earth itself behaves as though it were a giant magnet. The magnetic poles are not in the same positions as the real poles, so that a compass needle will point to 'magnetic north' rather than true north. The magnetic poles also move slowly around, and it also seems that at times during the Earth's history the north and south magnetic poles have changed round – so that there have been periods when a compass needle would have pointed south.

What we call 'solar wind' is made up of electrically-charged particles coming from the Sun. Some of these particles are trapped by the Earth's magnetic field, and move to and fro between

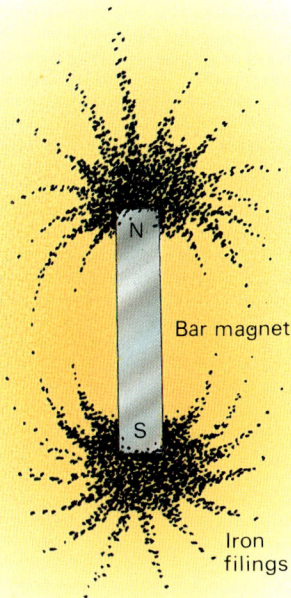

Iron filings come to rest along the magnetic field lines of a bar magnet.

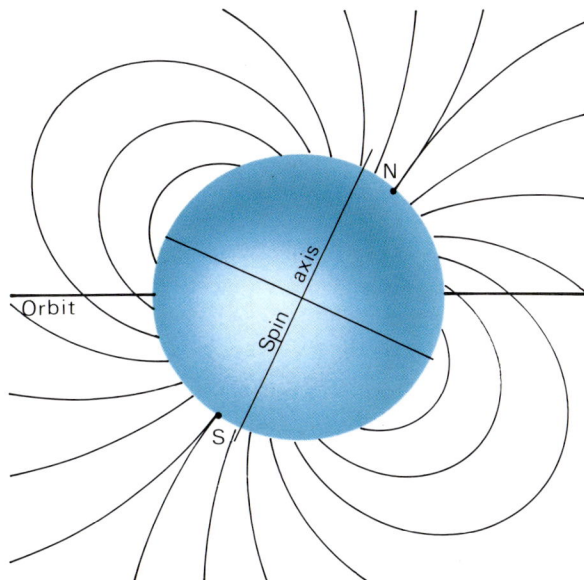

The magnetic field lines of the Earth follow the same pattern as those of the bar magnet.

the magnetic poles. Artificial satellites have told us that there are two belts of charged particles high above the Earth, one between 600 and 3000 miles (1000 and 5000 kilometres) and the other between 9000 and 15,000 miles (15,000 and 25,000 kilometres). They were first detected by instruments carried in the American satellite *Explorer 1*, in 1958. We call them the Van Allen zones, because the instruments in *Explorer* were designed by James van Allen.

When the solar wind is particularly strong, so many of these charged particles reach us that the Van Allen zones cannot hold them all. Some of them plunge downward toward the magnetic poles, causing the lovely glows which we call auroræ or Polar Lights – Aurora Borealis in the northern hemisphere, Aurora Australis in the southern. Auroræ are seen during most nights in places such as Norway, North Canada and North Scotland, but in England, which is further away from the magnetic pole, they are less com-

mon. However, we have brilliant displays now and then – as on 13 March 1989, when a splendid aurora was seen over the whole of the British Isles.

The Earth is not the only world to have a magnetic field, and indeed some of the planets in the Solar System have fields which are much stronger than ours. On the other hand the Moon, which has no liquid iron-rich core of the same kind as that of the Earth, has almost no magnetic field at all. If you ever go to the Moon, you will find that your magnetic compass will not work.

A very strong solar flare caused this beautiful aurora on 13 March 1989.

CHAPTER 19
THE EARTH'S MOON

We usually think of the Moon as being one of the most important bodies in the sky, but this is not really true. It shines brilliantly only because it is so close to us. It is much smaller than the Earth; represent the Earth by a tennis-ball, and the Moon will be no larger than a table-tennis ball.

The Moon has no air, because its weak gravitational pull meant that it was unable to hold on to any atmosphere it may once have had. The sky there is dark even in the middle of the day – and if you go to the Moon, you will find that you have only one-sixth of your usual weight!

Because the Moon has no light of its own and only reflects that of the Sun, it shows regular *phases*, or changes of shape. The diagram explains what happens. When the Moon is in position 1, its dark or night side is turned toward us; since this side does not shine we cannot see it at all – and this is what is known as new moon. As the Moon moves along in its path, a little of the sunlit side begins to face us, so that we see it as a crescent in the evening sky. By the time the Moon has reached position 2 it has grown to half-phase; it then becomes 'gibbous' (between half and full), and by the time it has reached position 3 the whole of its sunlit side is turned in our

The relative positions of the Sun, the Moon and the Earth during (*below*) solar and lunar (bottom) eclipses.

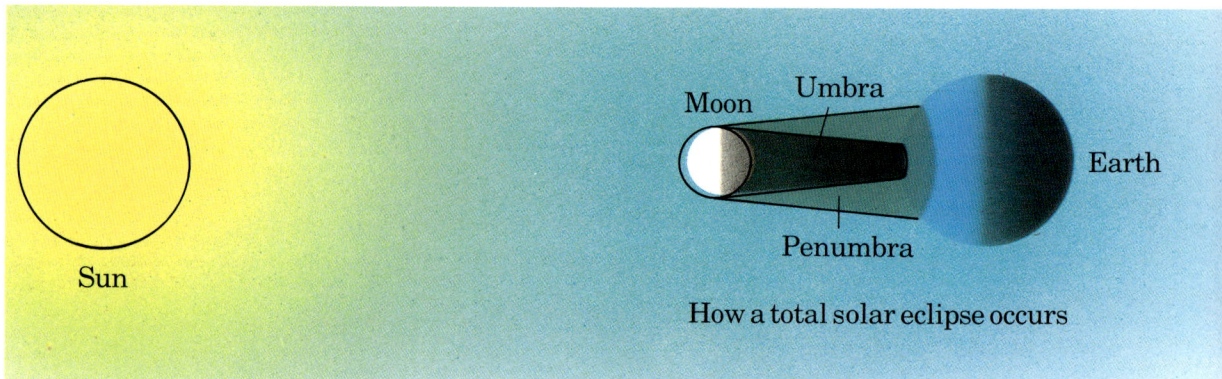

How a total solar eclipse occurs

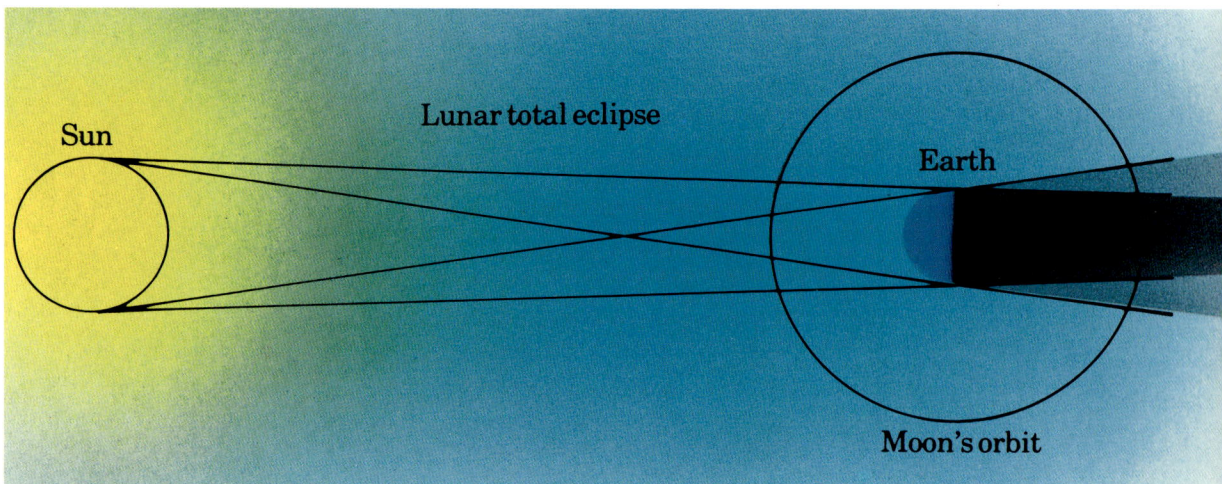

Lunar total eclipse

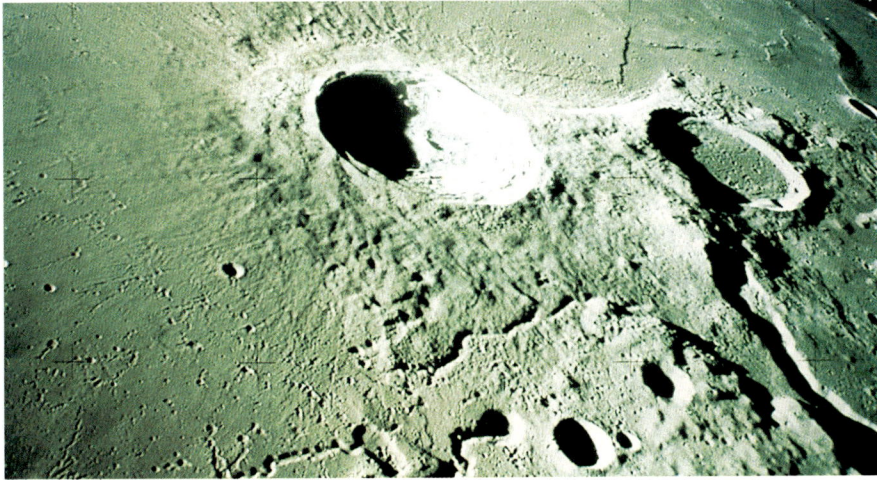

The surface of the Moon seen from the landing craft of *Apollo 15*.

direction. After full, it becomes gibbous again; then half (position 4) and back to new. The Moon takes just over 27 days to go round the Earth, but the interval between one new moon and the next (or one full moon and the next) is $29\frac{1}{2}$ days, because the Earth and the Moon are moving together round the Sun. Generally we have one new moon and one full moon in every month.

When the Moon is new (position 1) it is almost between the Sun and the Earth. If the lining-up is exact, the Moon blots out the brilliant disk of the Sun for a few minutes, causing what is called a solar eclipse. The sight is beautiful; when the Sun is completely hidden, at a total eclipse, we can see the solar atmosphere, together with masses of red hydrogen gas rising from the Sun's surface. It is fortunate that the Sun and the Moon appear almost exactly the same size in the sky. However, total solar eclipses do not happen often as seen from any particular place. The last to be visible from England was that of June 1927; the next will be on 11 August 1999, when you will have to go to Cornwall.

The Earth casts a long shadow in space, and when the Moon passes into the shadow, at a lunar eclipse, its supply of direct sunlight is cut off. The Moon turns a dim, often reddish colour until it comes out of the shadow again. At most lunar eclipses the Moon does not disappear completely, because some of the Sun's rays are bent on to its surface by the layers of atmosphere round the Earth. Lunar eclipses last for much longer than eclipses of the Sun, and they are more often seen, but they are not nearly so striking.

The Moon is a world of mountains, valleys, craters and dark plains which are called 'seas' even though there has never been any water in them; they were once filled with lava, so that there must have been great volcanic activity there. Some of the mountains are very high, and the largest craters are well over 150 miles (240 kilometres) across.

The first men reached the Moon in July 1969, when Neil Armstrong and Edwin Aldrin, from the space-craft *Apollo 11*, stepped out on to the lunar rocks. As expected, they found no living things; there has never been any life on the Moon. But before long there will be more missions there, and if all goes well there may even be a permanent Lunar Base before the year 2000.

43

CHAPTER 20

THE EARTH IN THE FUTURE

We have looked at the story of the Earth, and we have seen how it has changed since it was formed over four and a half thousand million years ago. What will happen to it in the future?

One thing is certain: the Earth will not last for ever, because of changes taking place in the Sun. As we know, the Sun is sending out light and heat because it is using hydrogen as a 'fuel', but when the supply of hydrogen begins to run out the Sun will shrink and become hotter. In perhaps 3000 million years from now the Sun will be so powerful that the temperature on the Earth will rise by at least a hundred degrees, so that the oceans will boil away.

Worse will follow. Over the next 250 million years or so the Sun will turn into a red giant star, with a diameter of at least 8,000,000 miles (13,000,00 kilometres); it will be 50 times as luminous as it is now, so that the Earth's surface will become a sea of molten lava. By then, of course, all life will have been wiped out.

This massive red giant star has used up nearly all of its hydrogen, and has destroyed any planets that may have orbited around it.

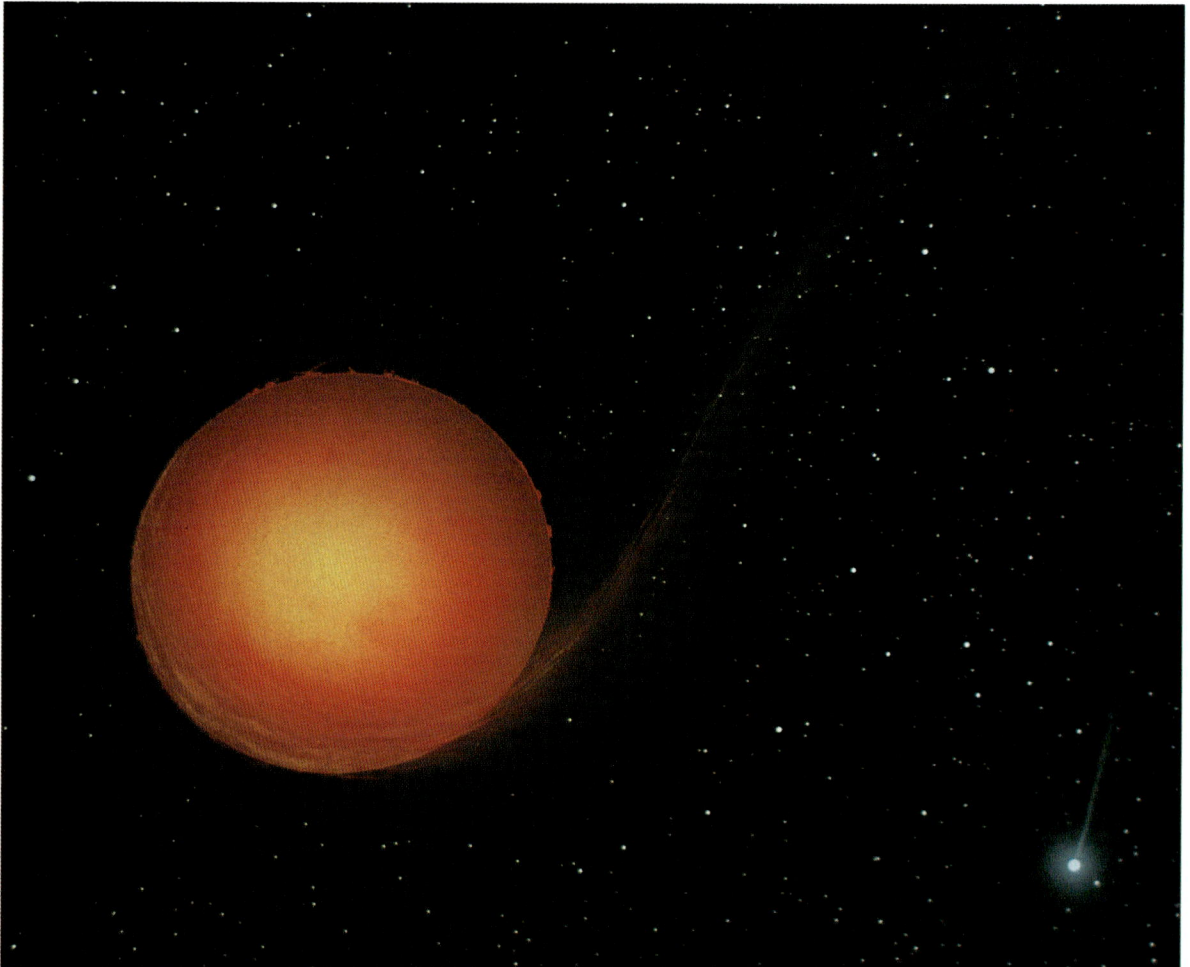

When the Sun is at its most powerful the Earth may well be destroyed altogether, and certainly there can be no hope for the inner planets, Mercury and Venus. Next the Sun will blow off its outer layers, leaving only a very small star, so dense that a spoonful of its material would weigh several tons. Stars of this kind are known as white dwarfs. Plenty of them are known; they are very old, and they have used up all their supplies of energy, so that they will end up as cold, dead globes.

This is bound to happen to the Sun,

In thousands of millions of years' time our Sun will die and become a small, dead star, like the one silhouetted in the foreground.

but at least there is no need for us to worry abut it, because there will be no obvious change for well over a thousand million years yet – probably longer. By then we may have learned enough to save ourselves, perhaps by leaving the Earth altogether and travelling to a planet in another star-system. The end of the Earth need not mean the end of mankind.

At present, then, the only real danger is that we may damage the Earth either by nuclear war, or by putting too much carbon dioxide into the air, or by destroying the ozone layer with our chemicals. Let us hope that this does not happen. The Earth is our home; we must take good care of it.

TEST YOUR SKILL

Try to answer these questions. You will find all the answers in the book, but do your best before looking them up on page 48.

1. Why is it summer in Britain when the Earth is at its greatest distance from the Sun?

2. How does the element uranium help us in measuring the age of the Earth?

3. Why is the sky blue?

4. Do we have spring tides or neap tides at the time of new moon?

5. Put the following geological periods in the correct order, beginning with the earliest: Permian, Jurassic, Pleistocene, Devonian, Carboniferous.

6. If you could drop Mount Everest into the deepest part of the Pacific Ocean, how much of it would stick out above sea-level?

7. What is the cause of an eclipse of the Moon?

8. Why was the present North Sea dry during the last Ice Age?

9. Which city was almost destroyed by an earthquake in 1923?

10. What is a Leap Year?

11. How long ago did the dinosaurs die out?

12. Why did the Earth's air change after plants spread on to the land?

13. What is, or was, an eohippus?

14. Why did men of the Old Stone Age use flint to make hand axes?

15. What is the latitude of (a) the equator, (b) the South Pole?

16. When the isobars on a weather map are close together, are the winds likely to be strong or gentle?

17. Why has the volcano Mauna Kea, in Hawaii, become extinct?

18. Gondwana and Laurasia joined together to make up one super-continent. What was its name?

19. What happened to the city of Pompeii in the year AD 79?

20. How do earthquakes help us to find out the size of the Earth's liquid core?

ANSWERS

1. Because the Earth's axis is tilted at an angle of $23\frac{1}{2}$ degrees, and during northern summer it is the Earth's northern hemisphere which is tipped toward the Sun.

2. Because it changes slowly into a special kind of lead. If we find uranium and uranium-lead together, the amount of lead tells us how long the uranium has been there.

3. Because the Earth's air scatters around the blue part of the Sun's light.

4. Spring tides, because the Sun and the Moon are pulling in the same direction.

5. Devonian, Permian, Carboniferous, Jurassic, Pleistocene.

6. None of it. The whole of Everest would be covered by water.

7. A lunar eclipse is caused when the Moon passes into the shadow cast by the Earth.

8. Because much of the world's water was frozen in the form of ice, and the sea-level dropped. When the ice melted the sea-level rose again, and the North Sea was flooded.

9. Tokyo, the capital of Japan.

10. A year in which February has 29 days instead of 28.

11. About 65 million years.

12. Because plants take in carbon dioxide, and give out free oxygen.

13. An ancestor of our modern horse.

14. Because flint is hard, but is also easy to chip into any required shape.

15. (a) 0 degrees. (b) 90 degrees South.

16. Strong.

17. Because it has moved away from the 'hot spot' in the Earth's crust.

18. Pangea.

19. It was destroyed by an eruption of Mount Vesuvius.

20. Because some kinds of earthquake waves (the S waves) cannot pass through liquid.